THE HASTINGS OF BOYLSTON, MASSACHUSETTS

THE HASTINGS OF
BOYLSTON, MASSACHUSETTS

GORDON H. HASTINGS

ISBN: 1539532844
ISBN 13: 9781539532842
Library of Congress Control Number: 2016917472
CreateSpace Independent Publishing Platform
North Charleston, South Carolina

TABLE OF CONTENTS

PROLOGUE

This writing is by no account an attempt to glorify the Hastings family name. My New England ancestors would have none of that. Quite to the contrary, it is born of the desire to commit to writing an answer to an often-asked question: *Where did I come from?*

I am fortunate that some of what you will read in this narrative comes from oral history around the family supper table and what I remember from listening to my brother and sister and aunts and uncles and neighbors reminisce. Most of this story is derived from hours of research into deeds and land records dating back to the 1600s. Many hours were spent with old books, newspaper articles, and interviews.

A humble mildewed cardboard box that stayed in our basement for countless years was filled with treasure. The water-stained documents and faded pages contained therein stimulated my imagination. The box of old photos of people I didn't know was kept in my parents' bedroom dresser drawer where the winter woolens were stored. The pictures of grandfathers, grandmothers, and those who came before them still smell of the mothballs.

Fortunately, many of the old buildings I write about here remained standing during my sister's, brother's and my young adulthood. The descriptions of old roads, streams, and ponds derived from my memories add further texture to this writing. During my childhood Boylston remained a rural community to the extent that many of the old roads were dirt cart paths with grass sprouting in the center. Rusted horse-drawn farm implements were scattered in overgrown fields. An ancient, giant Fordson iron-wheeled tractor lay abandoned where it belched its last breath. Small trees, more like brush, penetrated the metal driver's seat. Old decaying and weathered barns still stood.

My early ancestors were not diary keepers or writers of letters. They were farmers, men and women working from sun up to sun down, leaving little time for leisure. Details of their personalities are sketchy and anecdotal, but crafting this narrative allowed me to differentiate among them and to learn how they lived, who they married, and about their offspring.

Many of the old photographs included here are cause for both joy and concern. The joy derives from the thoughtfulness of those who placed these old and earlier studio portraits in safekeeping. The concern comes that in our digitized world, family photographs may disappear with a discarded cell phone or an accidental deletion. Who in today's digital world is a designated keeper of the sacrosanct cardboard box?

If you are a casual reader of this narrative, I hope that you take from this family history urgency to write yours. Don't rely on "File Save," but rather click "Print" and gather the pages. Download selected family photos from your cell phone, have them professionally printed and do not forget the captions. Find a large box with a fitted top, and fill it with these treasures. Over the years the mildew will only add to the thrill and authenticity of someone someday discovering *your* family history.

THE HASTINGS CREST

Motto: *In Veritate Victoria*
In Truth There Is Victory

DEDICATION

This work is dedicated to Thomas Hastings, who arrived in the New World from England in 1634; to his son Samuel (1665–1723); and to the nine generations of Hastings who contributed greatly to the family's way of life in Boylston, Massachusetts, from 1724 to 2002. I remain in awe of their devotion to family, community, and the land.

ACKNOWLEDGMENTS

The author is grateful for the research of Lowell Canovitch, husband of Marianna Hastings Canovitch, who through hours of labor provided many historical details and documents from which this narrative was crafted. I am also indebted to Calvin B. Hastings, who contributed greatly in sorting through property deeds and records dating back nearly three hundred years.

The genealogical account of Lydia Nelson Hastings Buckminster, published in her *Hastings Memorial* in 1896, provided an invaluable resource. I am also indebted to the Boylston Historical Society for the preservation of the writings and research of George Wright and William O. Dupuis.

A special thank you to Lynn Hastings, Calvin and Marrit Hastings, Gordon Calvin and Ragan Hastings, Alexandra Hastings, Brandt and Brooke Hastings, Erik and Megan Hastings and Dwight and Christine Hastings for their enthusiastic support of this research and writing.

The archive of historical materials prepared by Lowell Canovitch along with the original manuscript of this narrative is available to the public by appointment at the Boylston Historical Society, Boylston, Massachusetts.

Chapter 1

ENGLAND

I will never know exactly why Thomas and Susannah Hastings came to the New World. I do know that Thomas and Susannah were people of enormous courage who undertook a profound gamble to seek and find a better life in America.

"Thomas Hastings was of noble birth by descent from the family of Henry Lord Hastings, Earl of Huntington."

"The name Hastings is illustrious in history; and the race to which it applies is Danish in origin. In the early days of the British Kingdom, the Danes made frequent incursions upon that part of England and Scotland bordering the North Sea. It was in one of those incursions that Hastings, A Danish Chief, made himself formidable to Alfred the Great, by landing a large body of men upon the coast. He took possession of a portion of Sussex; and his family held the Castle and seaport when William the Conqueror landed in England; and they held it from the Crown for many generations."

"The first of the family who enjoyed the peerage was Henry Lord Hastings, son of William de Hastings, steward of Henry II. They were allied by marriage to the royal families of Scotland and England. King Henry VIII, in 1529, created Henry the Third Lord Hastings, Earl of Huntington. Sir Henry and George Hastings, grandsons of the Earl of Huntington, had sons, including Thomas Hastings who became Puritans, and were obliged by persecution to leave their native land and find homes in the New

World. Thomas Hastings was a great-great-grandson of the Third Earl of Huntington, Henry Lord Hastings 1536–1595."

(The above historical background is taken from Lydia Nelson Hastings Buckminster, The Hastings Memorial: A Genealogical Account of the Descendants of Thomas Hastings of Watertown, Massachusetts from 1634–1864 *[Boston: Samuel E. Drake, 1866].)*

Chapter 2

THE GREAT MIGRATION

England's King Charles I earned the dubious distinction of creating the impetus for the Great Migration to America, which brought the Hastings ancestors to the New World. In 1629 Charles I dissolved the British Parliament and began throughout England what historians have described as eleven years of tyranny including the persecution of those holding religious beliefs different than his (the Church of England) and especially those who identified themselves as Puritans.

John Winthrop was an English Puritan lawyer who had been born into a wealthy landowning and merchant family in Suffolk. As each month of the religious crackdown of Charles I passed, Winthrop became extremely anxious about his own family and the fate of those others who shared his beliefs.

Winthrop was aware of the Massachusetts Bay Colony created in 1628 by English settlers. He had also followed the success of William Bradford's Pilgrims and the Plymouth Colony founded in 1620. He drew a direct correlation between the Pilgrims quest for religious freedom and the current plight of the Puritans in East Anglia.

During the 1620s East Anglia was a hotbed of the Puritan movement and suffered mightily at the hands of the enablers of King Charles I. The region was also in the depths of a severe economic depression, and crop failure was rampant.

Winthrop spent two years during the despotic reign of Charles I organizing what historians later named the Great Migration. In 1630 from his flagship *Arabella*,

Winthrop led the first Great Migration fleet of eleven ships and eight hundred followers heading for a new life in the Massachusetts Bay Colony. In the ensuing ten years, an additional twenty thousand, including the ancestors of the Hastings family, would follow.

East Anglia, England, where Thomas and Susannah embarked from the port of Ipswich aboard the sailing ship *Elizabeth*.

Thomas Hastings was of noble birth. In 1866 Lydia Nelson Hastings Buckminster, writing in the *Hastings Memorial*, documented nineteen English peerages in the Hastings family name that had existed over many centuries. A peerage was a noble rank denoting wealth and large tracts of land. Buckminster wrote in the *Hastings Memorial* that 236 years after Thomas Hastings left England, three Hastings peerages remained, indicating that Thomas indeed disavowed a noble rank. Buckminster's research of 1866 found that there were then no discernable heirs remaining in England to bear those titles.

Thomas Hastings abandoned the potential of great wealth from a peerage through the lineage of Lord Hastings, Earl of Huntington. As the oldest male in the line, Thomas would have become the second Lord Hastings, Earl of Huntington. Instead, Thomas became enthralled with talk among his Puritan brethren of the New World, where there was religious freedom and individual economic opportunity.

Thomas Hastings, age twenty-nine, and his wife, Susannah, age thirty-four, resided in the large agricultural area north of London called East Anglia. The date of their marriage and how they met is unknown. It was unusual for a male living in that period of time to marry a woman five years his senior. Susannah's maiden surname is thought to have been Woodward. There is no evidence that Thomas married Susannah for either wealth or status.

On April 10, 1634, Thomas and Susannah, having signed an oath pledging allegiance to England, boarded the sailing ship *Elizabeth* at Ipswich, and set sail for America. They were among 108 men, women, and children crowded aboard the vessel. The majority of the passengers were fellow Puritans, also from East Anglia. They were part of the first wave of some thirty thousand who sailed to America during the Great Migration. His younger brother John would join him in the New World four years later. It is interesting to note the number of persons with the surname Woodward who sailed on the Elizabeth. Some of them may have been Susannah's relatives. *(Anne Stevens of packrat-pro.com compiled passenger list research of the 1634 sailing of the* Elizabeth.*)*

The Great Migration ship *Elizabeth* in 1634 carried Thomas and Susannah Hastings and 106 others to the New World. Among the passengers were families with as many as seven small children. Departing Ipswich at the same time was a second Great Migration ship named the *Francis*. The voyages of both the *Elizabeth* and *Francis* lasted about a month longer than the average seventy-five-day sailing time to the New World. One account of the voyage indicated that both ships were buffeted by heavy storms and were forced to put in for repairs at the Scilly Islands in the Caribbean. Another account states that six persons aboard the *Elizabeth* died during the journey and that many suffered from scurvy.

The Master of the *Elizabeth* was William Andrews. The ship proceeded from Ipswich Harbor into the English Channel, taking the southern route to the Atlantic Coast of North America. In the 1630s ships that could sail a more direct line to North American from England had not yet been designed.

Reaching open ocean, Andrews directed his helmsman to head southwest past the Azores and then turn west and then northwest toward the Massachusetts Bay Colony. In those days the average sailing time from England across the Atlantic to America was seventy-five days. Under normal conditions the *Elizabeth* would have been capable of sailing 100 to 150 miles per day, depending upon the favorability of the winds.

Weighing 180 tons and carrying 108 souls including a crew of 20, the *Elizabeth* was among the larger Great Migration ships. It was comparable in size to the *Mayflower*. The brave and adventuresome passengers aboard the *Elizabeth* brought with them only necessary personal possessions. The ship also carried cattle, pigs, chickens, sheep, and food supplies for sustenance on the journey and in the new land. Unlike the Pilgrims, these passengers had the advantage of knowing that earlier travelers, including John Winthrop in 1630, had established a successful colony at Massachusetts Bay. When the Pilgrims and William Bradford landed on Cape Cod in 1620, it was much more difficult because there was no English settlement and they were greeted only by wilderness and the Native Americans.

Every available space on the ship was used for transport, and there was little or no privacy on board. One can only imagine the difficulty of the voyage in such cramped quarters, without staterooms, bathroom facilities, or dining amenities. During all trans-Atlantic crossings, there usually was loss of life among the passengers from disease. Because Thomas and Susannah Hastings traveled without children, their voyage may have been easy as compared to Bridget and Humphrey Bradstreet, who boarded the *Elizabeth* with four children ages one to nine, three of them being under four years old. Another family, the Kemballs, made the voyage with seven children, all of them under the age of fifteen. Records show that they all survived the journey.

The voyage of Thomas and Susannah Hastings ranged from periods of boredom escalating to hours of terror. Traveling to the West from Europe required ships to tack into the wind. The *Elizabeth* rolled constantly from starboard to port. Huge waves crashed over the bow and rails. In the first days at sea, chroniclers of such voyages report, all on board were seasick, with only a bucket or the rail to relieve them. Many passengers lay in their bunks moaning.

The smells below decks were horrible. Goats, pigs, and horses were quartered next to the passengers. There was a common privy on the ship that provided little privacy, with a line often forming, adding to the indignity. Without children, Thomas and Susannah may have found it easier to escape to the ship's deck and spend hours at a time in the fresh air.

The *Elizabeth* and a second ship, the *Francis*, ran into heavy weather and were forced into port for repairs at Scilly Islands in the Caribbean. Having left Ipswich on April 30, the *Elizabeth* did not arrive in Essex, Massachusetts, located twenty miles north of Boston, until July 10. Captain Andrews, after several additional Great Migration voyages, permanently settled in the Massachusetts Bay Colony. One of his descendants would later live in Boylston.

Historians have well established that the success of the Massachusetts Bay Colony and the earlier Plymouth Colony was substantially due to the heroic migration of nuclear families such as those aboard the *Elizabeth*. They were bound together by their faith, and they brought with them the necessary skills, knowledge, tools, and work ethic to sustain life in the harsh New England environment. Unlike the early settlers at Jamestown, Virginia, the immigrants of the Great Migration, including Thomas and Susannah Hastings, were not fortune hunters but rather planned to propagate in the New World.

Chapter 3

WATERTOWN

After arriving in Essex, Thomas and Susannah gathered their few belongings and traveled southwest in a small coastal craft to Watertown, where they would settle. Why they chose Watertown is not clear. However, Governor Winthrop had become a puritanical zealot and word may have spread to the arriving ships about conditions in Boston. For a young couple that had fled the tyranny of Charles I, Watertown may have seemed like a better choice. Abundant fresh water and excellent farmland were prevalent in Watertown and it was easily accessible from the Atlantic by sailing inland upon what would later be named the Charles River.

Watertown was first known as Saltonstall Plantation. It was founded in 1630, just four years prior to the arrival of Thomas and Susannah. The original settlers, Sir Richard Saltonstall and the Rev. George Phillips, were thought to have been part of the group that sailed on the *Arabella*, the first of the Great Migration ships. Watertown was officially established on September 7, 1630, the very same day that the courts established Boston. When Thomas and Susannah arrived four years later, there were less than one hundred people in the community. Thomas's name is listed on the Founders Monument, which is located near Watertown Square on the north bank of the Charles River.

Thomas aggregated several substantial parcels of property. Later he purchased additional lots in Roxbury. He constructed a simple wood-frame homestead and then cleared the remaining land and built stonewalls to mark the boundaries of his property. During the colonial period, it took about one hundred acres to support a family. The house was located on what was then called Hill Street. Later he constructed a handsome larger house including a barn and several outbuildings.

Life in East Anglia had taught Thomas the skills of agriculture. In Watertown he planted orchards, vegetable crops, wheat for bread, and flax for clothing and assembled a small herd of milk cows along with pigs, goats and chickens. The heavy work was done with oxen that he purchased from a local farmer. His younger brother John left East Anglia four years after Thomas and joined his brother in Watertown in 1638, establishing his own homestead.

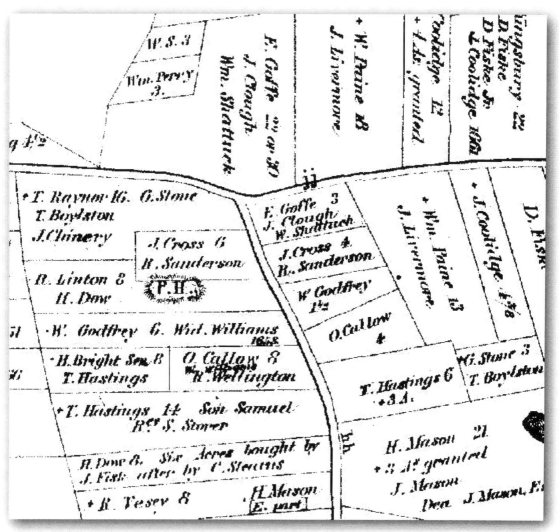

Early plot map of Watertown showing several parcels owned by Thomas Hastings.

For sixteen years Susannah and Thomas prospered, playing instrumental roles in the developing Watertown community. It was an agrarian society at the edge of what was then the colony's western frontier. The settlers raised their families, living self-sufficiently on small farms. Owning land was an essential part of the ethos of the colonists.

Susannah and Thomas were unable to have children. Susannah died in 1650 at fifty years of age, sixteen years after sailing from England, leaving Thomas as a forty-five-year-old widower. The cause of Susannah's death is unknown.

Shortly after Susannah died, Thomas met twenty-two-year-old Margaret Chaney, the daughter of William and Martha Chaney of neighboring Roxbury. The Chaney's were a prominent Roxbury family. Thomas and Martha courted for six months, and in the summer of 1651, Thomas asked her parents for their daughter's hand in marriage. Thomas and Margaret were wed in the Roxbury church in that same year.

The newlyweds moved into the Hastings homestead on Hill Street and over a period of thirteen years—from 1652 to 1665—had eight children—seven boys and one daughter. Thomas was forty-nine years old when his first child, also named Thomas, was born in 1654. Seven of their children outlived their parents, which was unusual in the colonies, where childhood disease and early death among infants was prevalent. One son, William, born in 1655, drowned in 1669 at age fourteen. Their only daughter, Hephzibah, married Deacon William Bond of Watertown and raised twelve children there. One of their children, Margaret, married into the Coolidge family of Watertown. The couple's sons John, Joseph, Benjamin, Nathaniel, and Samuel remained in Watertown.

Thomas and Margaret's oldest child, Thomas, was the first Hastings to leave Watertown. He had trained in medicine in Boston. In 1674 he traveled through the wilderness to the small town of Hatfield in western Massachusetts. There he established himself as a physician and enjoyed a distinguished career. He married Anna Hawks of Hadley and had six children, thus establishing the Hastings surname in western Massachusetts. He died there at age 60. His son Thomas Hastings Jr. also became a physician. Thomas' and Margaret's other seven boys including their youngest son, Samuel, born March 12, 1665, remained in the immediate Watertown area and established themselves on family lands.

Early military records show that Thomas and his brother John participated in King Philip's War during the Great Swamp Fight of 1675 in South Kingstown, Rhode Island with the Pequot, Mohegan and Narragansett tribes. King Philip was the American Indian chief Metacomet, who was the leader of the Pokanoket. Metacomet was the son of Massasoit the chief of the Wampanoag. Earlier the colonists had given him the moniker "King Philip." The Pokanoket were the American Indians that helped the original Pilgrim settlers survive their first winter in 1620. Later, American Indian tribes of the region were nearly annihilated by the English settlers during King Philip's War. Following the Great Swamp Fight, many of displaced tribes fled west to Mount Wachusett, a sacred American Indian gathering place, and others went further west, crossing the Hudson River.

Thomas Hastings was repeatedly called to leadership positions in Watertown inside and outside the church. At one time or another, he held virtually every office in Watertown including selectman, moderator and town clerk. His public service spanned five decades, and he was last elected to public office in 1680. Thomas was one of the town's most influential citizens; historians have called him one of the "old war-horses." Many of the surviving records from his time were written in his hand, and often government meetings were held in the Hastings home. He accomplished all of this while at the same time managing his two farms that supported an extended family.

Thomas and Margaret Hastings were people of means in the local society. In addition to the main homestead on Hill Street, Thomas owned two additional farms and another fifteen undeveloped lots in Watertown and Roxbury.

Thomas died in Watertown is 1685 at age eighty. Margaret predeceased him in 1678. There is no gravestone marking the burial location of either Thomas or Margaret, but it is believed they are buried in the Old Watertown Graveyard. None of the original Hastings homes in Watertown has survived. However, Hastings Street, where a family home once stood, is named after the family.

Upon his death Thomas Hastings's real estate was valued at 425 British Pounds, a substantial sum in colonial America. The homestead consisting of thirty-five acres along with an additional forty pounds passed to his youngest son, Samuel. Thomas distributed to each of his other children a sum of forty pounds. The remainder of Thomas's real estate was divided between his other living children. Samuel Hastings continued the direct line of ancestors that became the Hastings family of Boylston.

There are many well-known descendants of Thomas and Margaret Hastings. They include Anne Morrow Lindbergh the wife of Charles Lindberg, the world famous architect Thomas Hastings; the actress Carol Lombard; William Russell, Governor of Massachusetts from 1884 to 1887; and United States Vice President Richard Chaney.

A great-grandson of Thomas and Margaret, Lansford Warren Hastings, promoted the infamous Hastings Cutoff, a purported shortcut over the Sierra Nevada Mountains to California. In the fall of 1846, Lansford convinced the Donner Party to take the Hastings Cutoff, rather than the well-traveled Oregon Trail. The party set out destined to cross the Sierra Nevada Mountains before winter but learned too late that the Hastings Cutoff was not a shortcut. Forty-five members of the group perished after being marooned in the mountains by winter blizzards. The forty-eight who survived were forced to eat their horses, oxen, and dogs. Some were accused of resorting to cannibalism when food supplies were completely exhausted before rescuers finally reached them from California.

Chapter 4

SAMUEL HASTINGS

Samuel, the youngest son of Thomas and Margaret Chaney Hastings was born in Watertown on March 12, 1665. Samuel was one year from reaching his majority when Thomas died in 1685. John Nevinson of Watertown was appointed Samuel's guardian until his twenty-first year.

In January of 1687, having just turned twenty-three, Samuel married Lydia Church, the daughter of Caleb and Joanna Church of Watertown. Lydia died four years later in 1691 while giving birth to a daughter who survived for only one month. In April of 1694, Samuel married Elizabeth Nevinson, the daughter of John Nevinson, who had ten years earlier been his guardian. She died six years later in 1700. A year later in 1701, Samuel married Sarah Coolidge of Watertown, the daughter of Simon and Hannah Barron Coolidge. He remained in Watertown with Sarah to raise a family on his farm. He became the second Hastings to marry into the Coolidge family. His older sister Margaret had also done so.

In March of 1730, the court licensed Samuel to keep a tavern in Watertown but after a few years, he returned to the family homestead on Hill Street and continued farming as his full-time occupation. He followed in his father's tradition of community leadership, taking up several positions in the town.

Samuel and Sarah had six children, including Daniel Hastings, born on July 19, 1702, and his younger brother Nathaniel born in 1710. Samuel died in 1723 at age fifty-seven and is buried at the Old Burial Ground in Watertown. Daniel was twenty-one at the time of his father's death and was just married and living independently in Watertown. Nathaniel, the youngest child, was thirteen when his father died, and his mother Sarah raised him alone. She died ten years after her husband in 1733. Sarah is interred next to Samuel in the Old Burial Ground in Watertown.

By the time Daniel reached his maturity, tension over available land developed within the established families of Watertown. The best farmland had now been subdivided and distributed over three generations of the original settlers, including the progeny of Thomas and Margaret. Parents, including Samuel and Sarah, were finding it difficult to provide land and opportunity for their maturing children, which included Daniel's five brothers and sisters. Samuel's death was a major turning point in the destiny of the Hastings family. His son Daniel, now age twenty-three, was anxious to be in control of his own future.

The gravestone of Samuel Hastings, Nathaniel's father, as it stands at this writing in the
Old Burial Ground, Watertown, Massachusetts.

The gravestone of Samuel's wife, Sarah, is shown in the Old Burial Ground, Watertown, Massachusetts. She died in 1724 at age fifty-five. The identities of the two graves to the left are unknown.

Chapter 5

INTO THE WILDERNESS— DANIEL HASTINGS

(Author's note: The imagery of Daniel Hastings's journey from Watertown to Boylston is drawn from historical records and family anecdotal oral history unless otherwise referenced in the text. The actual description of the journey through the wilderness qualifies as historical fiction, there being no personal diaries from which to draw the specific details.)

Samuel's son Daniel, born in 1700, was the grandson of Thomas and Margaret Hastings. Daniel grew up on his father's farm in Watertown. He learned about husbandry, crop rotation, and the harvest from his father and from seasonal workers hired by the prosperous family. During his teen years, his daily chores on the farm were critical to the family because his father also operated a tavern. Daniel was mostly home schooled, with lessons taught by his mother. There were also lessons at the local church meetinghouse. Daniel loved farming and devoted himself to learning about breeding livestock and the various grains most suitable to the local climate. He helped his father develop the family fruit orchard, primarily apples, which was essential to a colonial family's food supply.

Life in Watertown for a young man was not all work. During his limited leisure, Daniel participated in social gatherings, usually involving the church. Daniel first met eighteen-year-old Sarah Ball at the meetinghouse. They saw each other often, always under her parents' supervision. The relationship blossomed, and at age twenty-two,

two years before his father died, Daniel asked Sarah's parents for permission to marry their daughter. The wedding took place on August 5, 1721, with a vast majority of the townspeople present to witness the union of two prominent Watertown families. His best man was his brother Nathaniel, who was eight years his junior.

Daniel and Sarah made their home at one of the two farms established earlier by Daniel's grandfather, Thomas. Children came quickly, with son, Daniel, born in 1722 and daughter, Betsy, in 1723. As his family and responsibilities grew, Daniel understood that the opportunity for expanding the farm and owning substantially more land in Watertown was limited, particularly because he had five other siblings.

Daniel learned from speaking with adventurers, traders, and trappers that forty miles to the west of Watertown was a small settlement located in a peaceful and fertile valley in a region called Shrewsbury and Lancaster. They also spoke of a place called Sawyer's Mill, established by the Sawyer family that included an operating sawmill located along a substantial river. They were told of fierce clashes between the Indians and settlers in that area. Legend was that in 1715, a member of the Sawyer family was taken hostage by local Indians but later was bartered for goods and returned unharmed. Most of the Native Americans fled the area after being hunted down by bands of Lancaster militia that set out in pursuit of them following the Sawyer kidnapping.

On August 5, 1724, one year after his father's death, Daniel, Sarah, and their two small children struck out toward the west in search of land and greater opportunity for their family. Daniel left behind his widowed mother, and his five brothers and sisters, including thirteen-year-old Nathaniel. The young couple abandoned the established, structured life in Watertown, where the family had first settled ninety years prior in 1634.

Daniel and Sarah loaded two horses with necessities, including clothing, cooking utensils, and as much nonperishable food as they were able to bear. Young Daniel, now age two, walked alongside his parents until he was exhausted, and then he and Betsy, age one, were carried. They trudged through a wilderness that the Neshoba, Asabet, Nashua, and Wachusett tribes had inhabited as recently as ten years earlier.

Daniel and Sarah rose at dawn each day, fed the children and themselves, and then pushed on westward. In many places the old Indian trail disappeared into the thick wilderness. In those areas Daniel blazed the trail with an axe in order to retrace their steps if for some reason they were forced to return. In the late afternoon, the tiny band of travelers would stop to seek a safe shelter for the night. They were fortunate if they were able to travel five miles in a day.

Daniel often constructed a lean-to against rock outcroppings providing a protective wall against the wind. The lean-to floor was covered with pine and juniper bows. In the first five days, they traveled twenty miles and passed through the last civilized settlement of Southborough, where they were given shelter and sustenance. Leaving Southborough they traveled further west along the same trail used by the Piquant in their escape to Mt. Wachusett following King Philip's War.

The Hastings travelers slept at night in their makeshift shelters beneath towering pine trees, often using the Indian fire pits they found for cooking and warmth. They ate hard tack and smoked meat they carried from home. Daniel would likely have shot turkey or pheasant.

Sarah nursed Betsy. Young Daniel was now old enough to share in the plentiful wild fruit they found along the way. Fresh water flowed from springs and streams, and to their good fortune, the weather—despite some rainy days—was mostly fair. They were lulled to sleep at night by whip-poor-wills but were occasionally abruptly awakened by the sounds of coyotes howling and the thrashing of black bears moving through the underbrush.

With the exception of a small settlement in what is now Northborough, the weary travelers did not meet another human in the fifteen miles and three days it took them to travel from Southborough to what would later become Boylston. They passed through Northborough and trudged upward along the old path leading to the west a portion of which would later be named Stiles Road. They descended upon a plateau where the land was level, and there were plentiful streams. Wild blueberries grew close to the ground on many parts of open land, particularly near outcroppings of ledge.

The family descended a small hill into a hollow. Daniel, Sarah, and the two children had just completed nine arduous days walking through the unbroken wilderness from Watertown. They had found the site of their new home.

There were no other settlers in the vicinity. Records detailing from whom Daniel purchased the property are vague, but the abutting landowners were named Bigelow, Jones, and Cushing. When Daniel's son David later bequeathed the property to his son David Jr. on October 9, 1798, the homestead had grown to contain nearly two hundred acres in two parcels. Also included was the two-story wood-frame colonial farmhouse located on Northborough Road (later named Central Street) that Daniel and Sarah had built in 1725. It remains today as one of the earliest structures built in Boylston and the very first in that section of the town. Daniel also built a large barn across the street, which incorporated a cider mill.

Daniel Hastings died on July 4, 1777, living to see the signing of the Declaration of Independence and the beginning of the Revolutionary War. Nine years after his death, the area he helped settle was incorporated in 1786 as the town of Boylston. Daniel's house and land passed to his ninth child, David Hastings, who continued to operate the family farm.

Chapter 6

NATHANIEL HASTINGS

Daniel was the first of the descendants of Thomas Hastings of Watertown to settle in Boylston; however, his younger brother Nathaniel Hastings is the first direct ancestor establishing a line of descendants leading to the creation of Maplewood Farm and to his great-great-great-great-grandson, Calvin Raymond Hastings.

In 1733 Nathaniel Hastings traveled alone through the wilderness from Watertown to his brother's homestead on the Northborough Road in what was then the Shrewsbury North Precinct. He informed Daniel and Betsy that he would soon marry and wanted to strike out on his own, as Daniel had done eight years earlier. There were now dozens of Hastings descendants of Thomas and Margaret Hastings populating Watertown, and Nathaniel—like Daniel—wanted his own homestead and the opportunity to become a large landowner.

Nathaniel purchased a ninety-four acre tract of land from Jonas Cuttoin and his wife, Diana. The purchase price was 237 pounds. Most of this land was in the fertile Nashua River Valley in that part of Boylston that at that time was called Lancaster. Nathaniel's homestead was located about two miles north of Daniel's. The actual home site sat high on a hill overlooking the Nashua River with Mt. Wachusett in the distance. Lying to the north in the valley below was Sawyer's Mill.

In the early 1700s, Joseph Sawyer had carved out a settlement along the Nashua River. Joseph Sawyer's ancestors also came to the New World during the Great Migration in 1636, two years after Thomas and Susannah Hastings. Joseph Sawyer's grandfather, a fur trader, did in fact settle in Watertown and would have been known by Daniel's grandfather, Thomas. Joseph Sawyer's father, Thomas Sawyer, also a fur trader, first discovered the Nashua River Valley while trading with the Nashaway tribe in the early1600s. Thomas Sawyer wrote in his diary a description of the Nashua River Valley and of the location of Nathaniel and Esther's future homestead:

"There lay spread out before them a beautiful interval clothed with nature's green carpet interspersed with flowers, with a silvery line of bright waters winding through the mist, the same now called Still River, mixed here and there with tall elms and hickory trees, they being the most hardy kinds of trees, and able to withstand the overflowing of the waters of the river during the spring and fall freshets. The table-lands above were covered with trees waving their green foliage in the breeze, and the lands being free of rocks and easy of cultivation, it seemed to them like a new Garden of Eden." *(From the diary of Thomas Sawyer as published in Armory Carter,* Sawyers in America *[Worcester, MA: Press of Edward R. Fiske, 1883].)*

W. RES. - BOYLSTON
STRIPPING ON SEC. 8, SAWYER'S MILLS
MAY 14, 1902

4347

Sawyer's Mills as photographed in 1902 just before the buildings were demolished to make way for the damning of the Nashua River and the construction of the Wachusett Reservoir. When the newlyweds arrived in 1735, the Sawyers were Nathaniel and Esther's closest neighbors. Daniel and Betsy lived two miles to the south. The original Sawyer's Mill buildings were much smaller and fewer in number. The Sawyer family was of tremendous assistance in helping Nathaniel and Esther establish themselves in what was then a wilderness.

Nathaniel Hastings and Esther Perry were married in Watertown on April 17, 1734, and departed for Boylston shortly thereafter. Settling there was easier for Nathaniel and Esther because they had as yet no children and his brother Daniel and his wife also provided a household and a base of operation while Nathaniel and Esther built their home.

Throughout the fall Nathaniel cleared the land, removed rocks, and burned stumps. The original house consisted of one large room with a fireplace and hearth and a separate bedroom on the first floor. Upstairs under the eaves was a sleeping loft. The doorway was in the center of the front of the house with windows on either side. Upon completion of the house, Nathaniel constructed a barn. Abundant fresh water came from a hand-dug well filled by a natural underground spring. Water flowed fresh and cold throughout the year. Nathaniel planted apple, peach, and cherry trees from cuttings he obtained from his brother. The family vegetable garden was planted just outside the rear entrance. The garden contained root vegetables that were conducive to winter storage.

Nathaniel had arrived in Boylston eight years after Daniel, but even then the area remained a wilderness. People marked trees to find their way to and from neighbors and the meetinghouse. Nathaniel and Esther's nearest neighbor, the Sawyer's house, was a mile away. Daniel's house was two miles in the opposite direction. The nearest doctor was eight miles to the south in the village of Worcester. It was a lonely existence, particularly in the brutal New England winters.

In a letter written by Rev. Dr. Cotton Mather to a friend in England, Boylston historian George Wright quoted:

"On the twenty-third and twenty-fourth of March, 1717 occurred the greatest snowstorm known in the history of New England, which was so violent that all communication was stopped and people for some hours could not cross from one side of a road to the other. Indians there nearly one hundred years old, affirmed that their fathers had never told them of any stories that equaled it. Vast numbers of cattle, sheep, and swine perished; some of them were found standing at the bottom of snowdrifts weeks after the storm. One farmer who lost 1,100 sheep found two of them still alive twenty-eight days after the storm at the bottom of a snow bank sixteen feet high having sustained themselves by eating the wool of their dead companions. Hogs were found alive even after being buried twenty-seven days. Hens were found alive after seven days, and turkeys after twenty-five days, in positions where they were utterly unable to obtain any food. Great damage was done to the orchards, the snow freezing to a crust as high as the branches broke and split them, and the cattle walking upon the crust greatly damaged them by browsing. Houses were completely covered with snow, not even the tops of chimneys being seen." *(George L. Wright,* Historical Phenomena from the Papers of George L. Wright, *(1884-1912, George L. Wright, Boylston, Massachusetts) trans. Amy Gilgis [Boylston Historical Society.])*

Nathaniel and Esther had six children while living at their homestead. Samuel was born in 1735; a daughter, Anna, was born in 1737; son Nathaniel Jr. was born in 1738; and son Thaddeus in 1740. Thaddeus departed for New Hampshire in his adulthood. Son Jonathan married Mary Fay of Northborough and remained in Boylston as a farmer. Nathaniel and Esther's youngest child, Silas Hastings, was born in 1746. Silas would inherit the family homestead upon Nathaniel's death. Conditions on the rural New England frontier remained extremely difficult for Nathaniel, Esther, and their young family. When Silas was only eight years of age, there was a serious health epidemic in the region.

Boylston historian George L. Wright wrote:

"There were thirty-seven deaths of children in neighboring Harvard, Mass. In 1752, a fever raged in Albany, N.Y., which carried away about forty-five people. It began in August and raged until it was checked by the frost of autumn; some physicians called it a nervous fever, but others the yellow fever. The bodies of some of the patients turned yellow. The crisis of the disease came about the ninth day, and if the sick survived that day, they had a good chance of recovery. The disease left the patients in a state of imbecility of mind, approaching children of idiocy. The following year there was an epidemic of dysentery in this section. In Sterling it was so fatal that one in every twenty of the inhabitants died within eight weeks of the first reported case. *(George L. Wright,* Historical Phenomena from the Papers of George L. Wright, *(1884-1912, George L. Wright, Boylston, Massachusetts) trans. Amy Gilgis [Boylston Historical Society.])*

It was fortunate that the children of Nathaniel and Esther and their neighbors were spared this epidemic; however, death from a future dreaded terminal disease would devastate the Hastings family two generations later.

Nathaniel Hastings farmed his ninety acres of land during the Revolutionary War. Foodstuffs from the farm were transported primarily to Dorchester Heights to help feed Washington's army as it executed the siege of the British in the city of Boston.

Not everyone in the colonial community was a patriot. The area was home to many British royalists, among them the Rev. Ebenezer Morse, the pastor of the Boylston Congregational Church. At the outbreak of affairs that led to the Revolution, Morse was found to be an unflinching royalist and so outspoken in his political sentiments that his parishioners, most of whom were strong adherents to the colonial cause, resolved to endure him no longer as their minister and asked him to resign. A purported gathering place for British sympathizers called the Tory Cave is located in the eastern part of Boylston adjacent to land that was owned at that time by Nathaniel Hastings.

There are no records or correspondence indicating the political leanings of Nathaniel during the time of the Revolution. Neither Nathaniel nor Daniel took up arms. A son of Nathaniel and Esther, Samuel (1735–1823), served as a captain in the Massachusetts Militia during the Revolution. Nathaniel Hastings Jr. (1738–1824) served in the Massachusetts Militia during the French and Indian War of 1754–1763. He is recorded as a corporal who marched with Colonel Oliver Wilder toward Fort William Henry in 1757.

Nathaniel and his son Silas played an important role in the establishment of Boylston as an incorporated town. Both men were appointed to a committee in 1780 to petition the town of Lancaster to separate that part of Lancaster where they had built their farmsteads and annex it to the Shrewsbury North Precinct where Daniel had built his home. Their argument was persuasive, and the leaders of Lancaster approved the plan. The annexation of the land included Nathaniel's ninety acres and became the present-day northern boundary of Boylston. Five years later in 1785, Nathaniel and Silas were part of the committee of citizens that successfully petitioned Shrewsbury to break off the entire Shrewsbury North Precinct, which a year later in 1786, was incorporated as the town of Boylston.

A year before Nathaniel died and two years after Boylston was incorporated, Nathaniel transferred his homestead on the Worcester Road overlooking the Nashua River to his son Silas, for which Silas paid him a sum of two hundred pounds. Nathaniel died a year later in 1789. The date of Esther's death is not recorded, but she must have predeceased her husband because she was not listed when Silas bought out his brothers. In a transaction dated January 18, 1790, Silas paid his brothers, Samuel, Nathaniel, Jonathan, and Thaddeus, a sum of 185 pounds as their share of Nathaniel's estate, and he became the sole owner of the original Nathaniel Hastings homestead.

Chapter 7

FATHER TO SON

Silas Hastings was born at the family homestead in Boylston in 1746. In 1776 he married Hannah Reed, also of Boylston. Hannah and Silas had thirteen children. Five boys and six girls lived to maturity. Two of their children died in their infancy.

Only one of Hannah and Silas's sons, Nathaniel, born in 1797, remained on the family farm. A Son Thomas lived to adulthood and died in Boylston. Son Ezra married and moved to Boston, where he died. Son Ephraim, born in 1785, married Ashsah Sawyer of Lancaster. Son Silas Hastings Jr., born in 1780, married Mary Andrews, daughter of Deacon Daniel and Dinah Andrews of Shrewsbury. Silas Jr. established the Hastings Tavern, located in Boylston Center at the intersection of Route 70 and Scar Hill Road. The building remains at this writing and is listed on the National Historic Register. Silas Jr. died in 1833 at age fifty-three. His widow continued living in the tavern, which was upon his death converted to a home. Dinah Andrews was related to Captain William Andrews of the sailing ship *Elizabeth* that brought Thomas and Susannah Hastings to the New World in 1634.

Silas and Hannah Hastings also raised six daughters. Daughter Hannah married Luther Ames and moved to West Boylston. Daughter Eunice married into the Howe family of Holden. Daughter Betsy married Stephen Pollard of Berlin. Daughter Mary married into the Fay family of Northborough. Daughter Martha married Joseph Flagg and settled in Berlin. Daughter Sally married Silas Howe and settled in Sterling.

Silas and his youngest son Nathaniel continued farming the original Nathaniel Hastings homestead on the Worcester-Clinton Road. The land located in the Nashua River Valley was extremely fertile. The acreage included the original fruit trees planted by Nathaniel plus field crops for the family's use, with any surplus placed for sale. Silas grew wheat, as did nearly all the colonial farmers in Boylston. He had his own milk cows, swine, draft horses and chickens.

The Hastings were instrumental in the formation of Boylston's first library. In 1792 the Boylston Farmers and Mechanics Association donated $50 to create the Boylston Social Library, a collection of some 350 volumes made available to the citizens of the community. It was the forerunner of what became the Sawyer Memorial Library.

Silas was very active in the affairs of the town. He served as town treasurer from 1823 to 1832. Five generations later his great-great-great-great-great-grandson, Gordon Hastings, would also serve as treasurer. Silas was also a selectman from 1825 to 1828.

By 1818, when Silas was seventy-two, his and Hannah's children had all reached maturity; some had married, and most had moved away from Boylston. Hannah was ten years younger than Silas, but in those colonial times, the sixties and seventies were considered old age. Decades of exhausting physical labor and child rearing took a heavy toll on early New England settlers. Large numbers of children were common.

Silas and Hannah decided they would sell most of the original homestead, retaining the house and a small plot of land for themselves. Eighty acres of the original ninety-acre tract were sold to Elikiem Moore for $2,556 on September 10, 1818. Silas died in 1833 at age eighty-seven and the original homestead was sold to a grandson, Charles Albert Hastings. Hannah died ten years later in 1843.

Nathaniel, the youngest of Silas and Hannah's children, remained in Boylston. He was determined to carry on the family farming tradition, even though the ancestral property was sold. In so doing, he would become the Hastings that began the legacy of Maplewood Farm.

The construction of the Wachusett Reservoir in Boylston as the primary new water supply for the city of Boston began in 1895. It was a project of incomprehensible proportion for the local residents. At one time there were five hundred men, mostly Italians, placing granite blocks one by one on the Clinton Dam to hold back the Nashua River. It took a year to fill the valley with water after the dam was in place. At that time it was the largest man-made reservoir in the country. The valley was flooded, and the reservoir was completed in 1908.

The original Nathaniel Hastings homestead and acreage was taken by the Metropolitan District (MDC) in 1901 to make way for the reservoir's construction. Charles Hastings, a descendant of Nathaniel and Esther, owned the property at the time. The homestead buildings ceased to exist. The Sawyer's Mill and homes and buildings in Sawyer's Village were torn down along with dozens of other houses, churches, barns, outbuildings, and small businesses to make way for the reservoir.

At the time of the taking of the land to construct the reservoir, the remaining Boylston farms, the largest of which were the Hastings Maplewood Farm on Central Street and the Stark Farm on Cross Street, played the major role in permanently creating a rural-agricultural culture that dominated the town in the first half of the twentieth century.

The remains of the foundations of the original Hastings house are present on a path leading across Route 70 from Hastings Cove at the Wachusett Reservoir. That portion of the road where Nathaniel's homestead was located was closed off in 1905, but the path, now a fire lane, continues past a metal gate erected by the MDC. Calvin Hastings, Dwight Hastings and Lowell Canovitch in 2001 discovered the old foundations of the house and barn as well as the hand-dug stone-lined well.

Calvin Hastings said, "We found the site by walking along the old roadbed looking for large trees. Sure enough, a short distance into the woods there appeared four sugar maples that were at least 200 years old. Beneath the outstretched branches were the foundations of the 1730s house and barn built by Nathaniel Hastings." Calvin added, "Those sugar maples would have had to have been planted by Nathaniel because all the other trees were much younger oak and swamp maple."

"We also found stonewalls that outlined the original fields, the walls being put up after the stones were removed from the areas where the crops were planted but no graves were discovered," Lowell Canovitch said.

Much of the original ninety-four acres of Nathaniel's homestead and farmland was located on the westerly side of what is now Route 70 and was flooded for the reservoir. Although care was taken by the MDC to relocate burial grounds, it is possible that the family burial plot and the graves of Nathaniel and Esther lie below the waters of the Wachusett Reservoir at Hastings Cove.

N. RES. S.W. FROM FRENCH HILL   79

This photograph is descriptive of the amount of river bottomland owned by Nathaniel and later his son Silas. Note the extensive fields that had all been cleared by hand and oxen. The Nashua River flows through the tree line at the west of the open fields.

N. RES. - BOYLSTON
SOUTHEAST FROM FRENCH HILL
NOV. 7, 1896

760

Another view taken of Nathaniel's original land photographed in 1896. The fence and stonewall in the foreground date back to the time of Nathaniel. Note the field crops in the distance surrounded by a crop of what is most likely hay and wheat. This land is now beneath the waters of the Wachusett Reservoir near Hastings Cove

WACHUSETT RES. BOYLSTON. WESTERLY FROM ENTRANCE TO
HASTING'S COVE TOWARD GREENHALGE POINT.   MAY 1918.   COMPARE WITH NO. 7293.   7294

Hastings Cove on the Wachusett Reservoir in a May 1918 photo looking to the west from French Hill,
showing much of the original ninety-four acres purchased by Nathaniel Hastings in 1734, now under
water. To the east of Route 70 on the higher ground across from Hastings Cove lie the foundations of the
original Nathaniel Hastings homestead, which remain at this writing.

Chapter 8

MAPLEWOOD FARM AND THE SECOND NATHANIEL

David Hastings Jr., son of Daniel and Sarah Ball Hastings, married Elizabeth Eager in 1792. She was the daughter of Joseph and Elizabeth Eager, who were also among Boylston's earliest settlers. The couple inherited the holdings of his father that included the original Daniel Hastings homestead on the Northborough Road.

In 1821 Nathaniel Hastings married David Hastings Junior's daughter Betsy Eager Hastings, his third cousin. Nathaniel was twenty-four years old, his wife Betsy twenty. They immediately set out to establish their own homestead, the Silas Hastings homestead having been sold by his mother and father three years earlier.

In 1823 Nathaniel and Betsy purchased from Thaddeus Chaney of Boylston forty-nine acres of land and buildings located on the Northborough Road a half mile further to the east of the original Daniel Hastings homestead. They also purchased from Chaney an additional twelve acres adjacent to the larger tract. There existed on the property a wood-frame house located on what would later become Green Street. Nathaniel and Betsy moved into that house and added a kitchen, barn, and workshop. The entire house consisted of two rooms on the first floor with two small bedrooms in the eves above.

Nathaniel faced the enormous task of clearing land to prepare it for cultivation. All the work was done with two teams of Belgian draft horses. Stone boats were constructed of thick oak planks and dragged along the ground where the large boulders and smaller stones of the rocky New England soil were rolled onto the stone boat, dragged to the perimeter of the future fields, and used to build stone walls that marked the boundaries of the farm. Some of the original Maplewood stonewalls built by Nathaniel remain on the property to this day. Two teams of horses were necessary in order to distribute the heavy workload. Nathaniel also kept a driving horse and a four-wheeled buggy for personal transportation over the undeveloped roads that had been the original footpaths through the wilderness.

The young couple farmed their newly acquired land and immediately started a family. Nathaniel and Betsy had six children, two of whom, Martha and Waldo, died before reaching their first year. Daughter Dolly was born in 1830 and son Eli in 1831. Daughter Betsy was born in 1833, and daughter Sophia was born in 1834. Nathaniel and Betsy quickly ran out of space in the small Green Street house, and they set about to build a large farmhouse and barn on Northborough Road that would later be named Central Street. At the same time, Nathaniel planted the sugar maple trees that created a magnificent foliage canopy over Northborough Road beginning at Hastings Brook just east of the barn and then westerly to the original homestead of Daniel Hastings. The mile-long arching rows of maple trees planted by Nathaniel became the namesake for Maplewood Farm. Many of the trees remain at this writing.

The new farmhouse was commodious. On the first floor were a kitchen, pantry and eating area, formal dining room, parlor, and single bedroom and adjacent bathroom in the rear. A wraparound covered porch surrounded the front of the house. Upstairs there were five bedrooms and a bathroom. The house was heated with stoves fueled with coal. The large kitchen stove used wood for fuel to obtain faster and hotter heat for cooking and baking. Nathaniel had never lived in so large a house.

The barn was connected to the house by a workshop. It was constructed so that a ramp driveway provided easy access for horses and wagons. Inside the barn were six large horse box stalls, separated by handsome lower finished planks and then ironwork that rose nearly to the ceiling. The doors were fitted with brass hinges and hardware. A cider press was located in a separate room.

Above the main floor was a large hayloft that included a modern laborsaving invention. A hayfork lift ran along a metal tract, and by using ropes and pulleys, large amounts of hay could be mechanically lifted into the loft by the power of one of the

Belgians drawing the ropes from the floor of the main barn. The loose forage was stacked in the hayloft, it being before the time hay bailers were invented. The mechanized hayfork was not the only modern invention adopted by Nathaniel. He constructed the first windmill in Boylston used to draw water from a deep hand-dug well located beside the barn.

Betsy's father, David Hastings Jr., a grandson of Daniel Hastings, had acquired from his father, David Hastings, large tracts of land in Boylston, including a parcel in excess of one hundred acres in the East Woods. When David Hastings Jr. died in 1835, Nathaniel and Betsy inherited one hundred acres, all of which was contiguous to the land they had earlier purchased from Chaney. Betsy's father through his bequest had contributed substantially to the expansion of the farm. Nathaniel and Betsy now owned a farm of in excess of 150 acres. The amount of work necessary to prepare this additional land for farming was enormous but was accomplished in less than five years.

Boylston farmers since the seventeenth century had established a tradition of apple growing. The climate had proved to be perfect for the crop. Nathaniel acquired the Walker Lots, property on high ground further to the east of Maplewood Farm. The land was accessed from the old Northborough Road that would a half-century later become Stiles Road. Here Nathanial began the farm's extensive apple orchards. The elevation of the land was about 650 feet, twice the elevation of where the farmhouse was located. The altitude was necessary to avoid the crop being destroyed by morning valley frost during the early spring blossoming of the apple trees.

Over a short period of time, Nathaniel assembled an enterprise that encompassed over 250 acres. It included the land gifted by Betsy's father, the Walker Lots, and a large forty-acre plot on Cross Street, which became the farm's south pasture for grazing cattle. When it was no longer in use as a pasture, it became the family woodlot.

Nathaniel now had enough land to support a larger dairy herd. The dairy business presented an expanded opportunity in addition to the abundance of field crops he was producing and marketing. People living in the city and those who no longer kept a family dairy cow were becoming dependent on bottled milk as well as fruits and vegetables purchased in stores.

Nathaniel constructed a second barn across the street from the main house. It was a large structure with a similar ramp driveway leading to the front doors. The new barn could accommodate forty dairy cows. In the rear was a storage shed for machinery, next to which was a silo. Above the barn door for the first time appeared a sign—"MAPLEWOOD FARM"—in red letters on a gold background.

In the early 1800s, the population of Boylston was about eight hundred people. There were more than half as many cattle. Nathanial Hastings was operating the largest farm in the community. During this period the Industrial Revolution was burgeoning in nearby Worcester, Clinton and at mills located along the Blackstone River Valley. These mills were making a variety of products ranging from nails to cloth, carpet, and even pianos. Demand for finished products was high, and wages at the mills were good. Many young men engaged in agriculture traded their hoes, cows, and horses for easier work and shorter hours in the factories.

Nathaniel Hastings was a contrarian. He correctly envisioned the coming market revolution in farming. Because so many had abandoned agriculture as a way of life, Nathaniel foresaw a booming market in providing milk, field crops, and fruit to the expanding populations in Worcester and as far east as Boston. It is interesting to observe that a great many of Daniel Hastings's descendants, Nathaniel's cousins, did depart from the family farm. By the end of the nineteenth century, the only Hastings remaining in agriculture in Boylston was the grandson of Nathaniel Hastings, who now owned and operated the flourishing Maplewood Farm.

Gravenstein, Baldwin, Russet, Crispin, Cortland, Idared, and Rome—all very hardy apples—were planted at the Walker Lots. They were perfect for growing in the New England climate and prime choices for cider. Closer to the house he planted the eating apples. These apples were bound for Boston, Worcester, New York, and England. There was a huge demand for cider during that period, and the cider apples were used to produce cider in Nathaniel's own mill for local sale. Brewers also purchased cider apples from Nathaniel to ferment into alcoholic beverages and to make cider vinegar.

At one time during this period, there were thirty cider mills within the town of Boylston including the large mill at the Hastings' farm. Nathaniel was the first

Hastings to hire a broker in Boston to purchase his apple crop at wholesale and then resell it throughout the area and overseas.

"In the year 1896 close to 1-million barrels of apples were shipped to England from the port of Boston. Many of those barrels of apples came from the orchards established at Maplewood Farm.

Boylston farms overall also produced not less than three thousand bushels of rye and about the same quantities of corn and oats each year. During the winter season the farmers carried large quantities of rye meal to Boston for which they realized the substantial price $1.25 per bushel." *(George L. Wright,* Historical Phenomena from the Papers of George L. Wright, (1884-1912, Boylston, Massachusetts), *trans. Amy Gilgis* [Boylston Historical Society.]

Tragically, in 1854, Nathaniel died at the family dinner table, choking on a piece of meat lodged in his throat. He was fifty-seven years of age. Overnight Maplewood Farm came under the stewardship of Betsy, his wife of thirty years, and Nathaniel's only surviving son, twenty-four-year-old Eli. Betsy had just turned fifty-three. Eli had worked by his father's side since childhood. Betsy never remarried and guided her young son in taking over the enormous responsibilities of the family enterprise.

The original Maplewood Farm barn constructed on Central Street was on the north side of the street attached to the farmhouse. The new barn constructed by Nathaniel on the opposite side of the street from the farmhouse is the structure to the left behind the sign for Maplewood Farm. Nathaniel's son, Eli, added the extension of the barn seen to the right when he expanded the dairy herd.

The canopy of maple trees towering over Central Street that was originally planted by Nathaniel Hastings in the 1830s. They became the icon of Maplewood Farm.

Chapter 9

UNDER ONE ROOF

Markets for farm goods abounded as a widower headed the family. While others left for factories and offices in the city, a twenty-four-year-old visionary seized the moment.

Two years after his father's death in 1856, Eli married Adelade Maynard of Northborough. They had eight children, three girls and five boys, including William Henry Hastings, born in 1860.

Eli Hastings, son of Nathaniel Hastings and great, great grandson of the first Nathaniel Hastings, who came to Boylston in 1734.

Adelade Hastings, the former Adelade Maynard of Northborough, married Eli Hastings in 1856 and settled at Maplewood Farm. Eli's mother, Betsy, was alive and also living at Maplewood.

Great sadness enveloped this large family at Maplewood Farm during the late 1860s and 1870s. Eli and Adelade witnessed the deaths of four of their five sons. Nathaniel Hastings, born in 1859, died of cholera in 1869 at age ten. Samuel A. Hastings, born in 1871, died in 1872 at age one, also of cholera. In 1873 an infant boy died at birth. In 1874 a fourth son, Charles M. Hastings, died at age one of lung fever. William H. Hastings, before reaching the age of twenty-seven, had witnessed the death of three of his four brothers and his mother. His older brother Nathaniel had died the year before he was born.

It is not known how Nathaniel and Samuel contracted cholera. There was a cholera epidemic in the United States in 1873, but it was primarily concentrated in Birmingham, Alabama. Cholera is highly contagious, and it is exceptional that no one in the family died of the disease other than the two boys. Ironically, there was no reported cholera epidemic in either Boylston or the state of Massachusetts in 1873. Though not recorded in family history, a seasonal worker may have brought the disease to the farm.

Eli's wife Adelade died suddenly of apoplexy in 1887 at age fifty-one. Eli never remarried. He was left to raise seventeen-year-old William and three surviving daughters, Lottie, Emma, and Dolly. Dolly Hastings, named after Eli's sister, married into the Mahan family of Boylston and lived until 1939. Emma married into the Winchester family of Worcester and lived until 1938. Lottie married in to the Burpee family of Lancaster and lived the longest, dying in 1964 at age 86. The sadness of losing a wife at a young age and the raising of the children left to the widower would repeat itself in the next century.

Throughout the 1860s, Eli Hastings expanded Maplewood Farm. He was young and energetic and was empowered by his father Nathaniel's optimism. He enlarged the orchards, cleared more cropland, and doubled the size of the milking herd. The largest expansion was the addition of a modern dairy barn attached to the large barn that Nathaniel had constructed across from the farmhouse in the 1840s. This relatively modern structure by the standards of the day contained a double row of stanchions and feeding troughs for eighty milk cows. The original structure was then used for hay and the storage of the large number of farm implements. The stalls for the draft horses and the cider mill remained in the barn attached to the main farmhouse.

In addition to farming, Eli engaged in the business of buying and selling livestock, mostly cattle. He prided himself on his herd of purebred Holsteins. In many cases calves and steers born at Maplewood Farm would be sold to other dairy farmers and to farmers that raised steers for the beef market. It was a prosperous business right up until Eli died and the farm passed directly to his only remaining son, William H. (Will) Hastings.

According to the census of 1870, Hastings family members living at Maplewood included Eli's mother Betsy, Eli, Adelade, William, and Adelade's daughters Dolly, Emma, and Lottie. Also living with them was Eli Sanderson, the seventeen-year-old son of Eli's older sister Dolly. Eli Sanderson's mother and father had died within a year of each other when he was ten years old. He stayed at Maplewood until 1877 when at age 23 he married. Also living at Maplewood Farm until she married Charles Fales of Shrewsbury in 1864 was Eli's twenty-six-year-old younger sister Tamah Sophia.

It requires little imagination to assume the amount of daily household work for which Adelade and Betsy were responsible. The farmhouse on Central Street was large, with five bedrooms upstairs and one downstairs. In addition to the large kitchen and pantry, there was a dining room and front room on the first floor along with a center hallway. A covered porch wrapped around the entire front of the house. Connected to the kitchen was a workshop, which led out to the main barn and cider pressroom.

Even with six bedrooms, the three girls plus Will and Eli Sanderson surely doubled and tripled in the bedrooms, allowing Eli and Adelade one for themselves. They also found space for his mother Betsy and sisters Dolly and Tamah. Some members of the large family and certainly any hired help lived in the old farmhouse acquired by Nathaniel Hastings when he bought the Chaney property on Green Street. Betsy moved from Green Street into the main farmhouse to help her son after Adelade died. Betsy died there twenty years later in 1874.

With a dozen people gathered for three meals a day, Adelade, Dolly, and Betsy rarely left the kitchen. There would also have to be additional provisions made for feeding the hired help at the noontime meal. Eli, as his son William would do later, hired extra help at planting and harvest time. The farm was not mechanized, and all the tilling of the fields and gathering of the crops was done with draft horses. The milking of the cows was done manually. Electricity did not come to that part of Boylston until the early 1900s.

The cooking was done on a wood-burning stove. The kitchen had its own separate entrance from the front of the house and additionally through the attached storage pantry and workshop leading to the barn. Fortunately, there was a windmill that pumped water to the kitchen sink, so they could avoid the trek to the well for water.

The lack of electricity also meant that all meals were prepared from mostly fresh food, except in the winter and early spring when the icehouse provided for storage of some meats and a large root cellar stored vegetables. Food from the farm was abundant, including milk, cream, eggs, fresh vegetables, pears, peaches, apples, cherries, and strawberries. From the garden came green and yellow beans, peas, beets and summer squash, turnips, cabbages, potatoes, sweet potatoes, corn, cucumbers, butternut squash, Hubbard squash, and onions.

Much to the children's delight, Eli also planted popcorn to be dried and used during the winter months. The farm also boasted a large chestnut tree across from the farmhouse near the driveway to the lower dairy barn.

Chicken and pork raised on the farm were abundant, and several beef cattle were slaughtered each year. Corned beef was made and stored in brine in crocks. All the fruits and vegetables not conducive to winter root-cellar storage were preserved in glass canning jars. The canning season began when the first crops ripened and did not end until applesauce and preserves were packed in the fall. The women of the household did all this work.

Bread was an important part of every meal and baked each day. All deserts including cakes and pies were made from scratch. Boston baked beans were a staple in New England farm family diets. Traditionally they were cooked overnight on Friday when the hot stove was not in use so that the heat was never wasted. In the early spring, gallons of maple sap from the maple trees planted by Nathaniel that lined Central Street would be boiled down to make maple syrup. Hot water for washing and personal hygiene was kept warm on the big stove.

During the Monday–Saturday workweek, the noontime dinner was always served to the family and hired hands around a large kitchen farm table. Sunday and all holiday meals were served in the dining room. Heating was provided in the living areas of the house by coal-burning stoves connected to a central chimney, which also allowed for a small stove in each of the upstairs bedrooms. The largest of these stoves was in the front room.

The firewood for the kitchen was cut during the winter months, allowed to dry over the spring and summer, and then cut by hand into stove-length pieces, which were drawn by horse and wagon to the house where it was stacked for easy access. Over forty cords of wood were required for a single season.

(Author's note: At this writing there remains one plot of twelve acres in the Boylston East Woods that was once part of Maplewood Farm. It is owned by the Hastings Land Trust and called the Hannah Sanderson Lot. It was bequeathed to Calvin R. Hastings upon Hannah Sanderson's death in recognition of the assistance that Eli Hastings had provided the Sanderson family in raising Eli Sanderson after his mother and father died. The property was not part of the sale of Maplewood Farm. Calvin B. Hastings, in later years formed the Hastings Land Trust in which the land is held as of this writing.)

Chapter 10

TWENTIETH-CENTURY MAPLEWOOD FARM

For generations the Hastings men and women tilled the soil, first with hoes and shovels, and then with oxen and horses. They prospered and enlarged the enterprise. The coming of mechanization and electricity changed the landscape forever.

William (Will) Henry Hastings was the sixth generation grandson of Thomas Hastings of Watertown. He was born at Maplewood Farm in 1860 and was the only one of the five sons of Eli and Adelade to live past the age of ten. He had three younger sisters, Lottie, Dolly, and Emma. From his early youth he worked at his father's side on the farm. He attended school through grade eight.

In 1885 at age twenty-five, Will married nineteen-year-old Arvilla Snow, who was born in Eastford Midway, Nova Scotia, Canada. The wedding took place in Raynham, Massachusetts, on March 7, 1885. Arvilla was the daughter of Ichabod and Lucy Snow. It is not known how or where Will and Arvilla met. After the wedding they settled at Maplewood Farm. Will's father, fifty-five-year-old Eli, lived with them in the family residence on Central Street.

Eleven years after they were married, Arvilla died in 1894 at age 28. She and Will had two children, Eli (Lee) Hastings born in 1887 and William Earl Hastings born in

1889. They were seven and five years of age when their mother died. Like his father, Eli, Will was now a widower left with the responsibility of raising young children.

In 1896, Will Hastings married Melinda Anastasia Tumblin, daughter of John Austin and Elizabeth Miener Tumblin. She was born on Tumblin Island, Nova Scotia, part of the LaHave Islands, which lie off the Atlantic coast of Nova Scotia one hundred miles south of Halifax.

Tumblin Island is a rocky land rising from the sea and covered with scrub pine. Long lining for codfish and lobster fishing were the main occupations of the Tumblin family. Melinda's older sister, Ida Tumblin, had immigrated to America and married Lawson Wright, a chicken farmer in the Morningdale section of Boylston. They're being few opportunities for a young woman on Tumblin Island; Melinda in the early 1890s joined her sister Ida in Boylston where she met and married William Hastings. Melinda immediately became the stepmother to Will's two young boys, Eli and Earl. Will and Melinda had two children together, Albert born in 1897 who died in his infancy, and Calvin Raymond Hastings born in 1900.

In 1906, Will, at age forty-six inherited Maplewood Farm upon his father Eli's death.

(Author's note: It is interesting that Will's first wife, Arvilla, was also from Nova Scotia. It is not known to the author whether there was a connection between the two women. Melinda was ten years younger than Arvilla, and Arvilla was not from the LaHave Islands but from the opposite side of the province in Digby County. It is coincidental that Will was the only surviving son of his father and mother and that Calvin R. Hastings was the only surviving son of William and Melinda. Both of the sons were to inherit the family farm from their father.)

This family photograph was taken in front of the Maplewood farmhouse on Central Street in approximately 1908. The old photo bore no identifications, but through deduction and cross-reference to other family photos, the identities were made. Back row (from left to right) Eli Hastings (Lee), William H. Hastings (Will), William Earl Hastings, Melinda Hastings, Emma Hastings Winchester (Will's sister), Dolly Hastings Mahan (Will's sister), Walter Edward Winchester, and Leon Winchester (Dolly's son). Front Row: Seated second from the left is Will and Melinda's only surviving son, Calvin Raymond Hastings, at age eight. The remaining children in the photograph, all seated except sixteen-year-old Leon, who is standing next to his father, are likely those of Dolly Hastings Mahan and Emma Hastings Winchester. The Mahan children were named Howard and Clarence. The Winchester children were named Harry, Bertha, and Phyllis. It is interesting to note the physical fitness of the adults, likely the result of the strenuous activity of daily farm life.

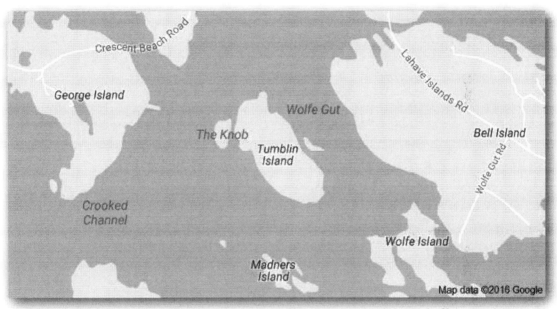

Tumblin Island, Nova Scotia, Canada, part of the LaHave Islands located off the South Atlantic coast of Nova Scotia.

Eli Hastings (Lee) was born at Maplewood Farm in 1887. The oldest son of Will and Arvilla and Calvin's half-brother, he lived and worked at the farm through 1920. He became an accomplished self-taught carpenter. Lee kept all the farm buildings in good shape and also worked for others in the community, building houses and repairing structures. Lee's work took him to western Canada in Alberta to build a frontier community there and, oddly enough, he also took a job picking apples. Census records show that he was back at Maplewood Farm in 1930. Later in 1937, Lee played a pivotal role in building a new home for Calvin and Elsa upon Maplewood Farm land at Central and Cross Streets. Lee's brother Earl, according to family lore, had little interest in the farm.

William Earl Hastings, born November 30, 1889, was the younger brother of Lee. Earl married a local woman, Edna (Lena) Wright, on April 14, 1914. He was twenty-five, and she was seventeen. Edna and Earl had two children together, William S., born in 1916, and Eleanor, born in 1917.

At the time of Earl and Edna's marriage, the old Green Street farmhouse originally occupied by the second Nathaniel Hastings and then briefly by Eli and Adelade was empty. Will Hastings deeded the house and three acres to Earl after Earl married Edna. The property included four large pear trees and several apple trees that had been planted by Nathaniel.

Edna and Earl's son, William (Bill) Hastings, born in 1916, lived at Maplewood Farm as a teenager with his Uncle Will and Melinda for an extended period of time. Bill's sister Eleanor (Ella), born in 1917, married Gilbert (Gil) Pratt in June of 1934 at age seventeen. A son, Paul, was born in 1937. Ella contracted tuberculosis and died in 1941 at age 24 when Paul was four years old. Paul and Gilbert lived for a while with Edna and Earl. After the Japanese bombed Pearl Harbor, Gil enlisted in the US Army. Paul stayed with his grandparents. Gil served overseas and was declared missing in action. Paul received a great deal of sympathy from the townspeople, having first lost his mother from tuberculosis and then appearing to have also lost his father. He often was seen wearing a children's size military uniform in remembrance of his father.

However, Gil Pratt was not missing in action after all. He reappeared in Boylston after the war and immediately sought to be reunited with his son. Edna and Earl by this time had raised Paul to the age of seven and saw themselves as the family that should continue his upbringing. With Gilbert Pratt's agreement, Edna and Earl Hastings gained custody of Paul and raised him until his adulthood. Paul retained the last name of Pratt, and he later married and moved away from Boylston.

Earl died on September 17, 1965, at age seventy-six. Edna continued living in the Green Street house until her death in 1970.

Will Hastings, like his father, Eli, was extremely enterprising. He had been working at Eli's side at Maplewood Farm since he was old enough to help and had learned every aspect of the enterprise. Upon taking over the farm when his father died, Will decided to get out of the livestock trade that Eli had established and focus all of his attention on expanding Maplewood into a modern dairy farm with over one hundred head of Holstein dairy cows. He also focused upon apple production and the growing of field crops for sale in Boston and Worcester.

The US 1900 Census records show that Will hired outside help to assist his new wife, Melinda. John Mills is listed in the census as a "full time servant." Eli died at Maplewood Farm in 1906 at age seventy-six. The cause of his death was listed as senility.

Maplewood Farm as it appeared circa 1920, the period in which Will Hastings took over the farm from his father Eli. The Maplewood farmhouse is in the distance. Note the new planting of the young fruit trees, all of which would later be destroyed during the 1938 hurricane. All the maple trees seen by the farmhouse along Central Street that were planted by Nathaniel survived the hurricane.

As a young boy, Calvin's entire horizon, just like his father's, was the family farm. It was likely that he was assigned daily chores by the time he was five years old. He first attended school in a one-room schoolhouse in the east end of town near the farm and then later at the Boylston Consolidated School in Boylston Center when the one-room schoolhouses scattered about town were closed. Like his father, Calvin matriculated through the eighth grade and began the long journey of working with his father full-time at Maplewood Farm.

Work on the farm was arduous. Calvin and Will rose before dawn and together with hired hand William Currier milked the dairy herd, a daily routine not completed until after 8:00 a.m. After milking, in the months of good weather, the herd was turned out to pasture for the day. The cows meandered back to the barn in the late afternoon, and the milking process began all over again. In the winter months, the herd would either be kept inside on bad weather days or on fair days be turned out into the rear barnyard where piles of hay were placed for forage.

The dairy barn was cleaned of manure in the morning and evening after milking. The manure was hoed through scuttles that dropped into the barn cellar. In the spring and fall, the manure was loaded onto horse-drawn manure spreaders and distributed over the pasturelands, the hayfields, and the produce fields. No artificial fertilizer was used at Maplewood Farm.

In the late winter, each apple tree required pruning to ensure new growth of budding branches. Pruning also kept the apple trees at a manageable height to allow access to the fruit at harvest time. It required an hour to prune each tree. Later, just after the apple trees blossomed and leafed out, all the trees required spraying twice yearly to prevent blister and disease. In the early years, the spraying was done by hand pump but became mechanized by the 1920s. The apple harvest took place in September and as late as October for the cider apples.

The amount of silage and hay that Maplewood Farm gathered and stored each year was enormous. A 1,000-pound Holstein daily consumes three pounds of hay and three pounds of grain for each gallon of milk it produces. The average cow at Maplewood Farm produced five gallons of milk a day and consumed at least sixteen pounds of silage and twelve pounds of grain. During the summer months, some of the cattle's daily forage came from grass growing in the pastures. In the summer the dry cows ready for the breeding cycle would be coupled with those from the neighboring Stark Farm and taken by drovers to pastureland twenty miles away in Princeton and then driven back to Boylston in the fall.

The majority of the hay and silage for the cattle was produced on the farm and stored in the main barn and in the hayloft in the original barn adjacent to the farmhouse. Additional hay was harvested from surplus fields of other farmers and carried back to Maplewood. The grain was purchased and stored in a large grain room on the main floor of the cattle barn.

During Will's stewardship the farm was the first in the east end of Boylston to have electricity and a telephone. With electricity came the arrival of the milking machine. Previously, Will or his son Calvin could hand milk a single cow in ten minutes, but the machine accomplished the milking in less than half the time. The milking machine made it possible for Will to double the size of the Maplewood Holstein herd.

Electricity also provided for refrigerated storage in the milk room, eliminating the need for ice and for immediate pick up by the milk processors. Maplewood Farm did not bottle its own milk, but there was plenty of raw milk and cream for the family to drink and use in cooking. The market for milk burgeoned as the neighboring city of Worcester grew. Maplewood Farm was among the most modern farms in Worcester County.

Despite farm tractors becoming available in the early 1900s, Will remained committed to his two teams of Belgian draft horses. They were a prized possession on a farm that had a long heritage of horses tilling the soil. The perfectly matched pairs of geldings stood at seventeen hands, and each weighed nearly 2,000 pounds. Both teams had been raised and trained by Will's father, Eli. The farm owned several wagons and three large sleighs for transporting goods in the winter. The farm also had a horse-drawn hay mower, manure spreaders, cultivators, sulky plows, harrows, and a wooden sledge used for moving large stones and other heavy objects. All the wagons and sleighs had "Maplewood Farm" in gold letters on a red background emblazoned upon the side.

Calvin Brandt Hastings remembers,

"I saw my grandfather holding the reins as the huge horses named Nat and Sam gently stepped down the ramp from the barn next to the house. He spoke to them in a language only he and the horses understood as they moved in a perfect rhythm. Guided across Central Street the horses would gently back up to the double sulky plow and stand perfectly still as my grandfather hitched the traces. He would then climb aboard the single metal seat and with a gentle clicking sound the horses would move out toward the field."

(Author's note: I recall my father, Calvin R. Hastings, reminiscing about his father and his horses. His thoughts are paraphrased here.)

"Will, my Dad, was slight in stature, and those Belgians were huge. I remember seeing him sitting on the dual sulky plow behind the team in the field. With the slightest whisper from my Dad, the horses' ears would flick forward, and in tandem they lowered their heads, leaning their big chests into the harness. The traces tightened, the leather squeaked, and the team moved forward in perfect unison. Rich brown earth flew from the sides of the plow blades digging straight furrows, exposing the sweet smelling freshly turned earth. At the end of the row, with another almost inaudible command, the Belgians turned by sidestepping and reversed direction with never a wasted motion. The reins lay loose in my father's lap."

"At the end of the day, Will removed the harness and the steaming horses stood still at the top of the ramp leading to the barn by the house. With a pail and large sponge, he carefully washed them and cleaned their feet with a hoof pick, always talking to them in a whisper. When the horses were put away, Will sat in the sun in the barn doorway on a three-leg milk stool and cleaned every inch of both leather harnesses, carefully polishing the brass knobs at the top of the two collars."

The first motorized tractor came to Maplewood in the late 1920s when Will purchased a Cletrac that ran on steel tracks and had a pulley on the front called a power take off. It was connected to the machine that chopped silage and blew it into the silos at the rear of the main cattle barn. The tractor was also used for much of the fieldwork.

Calvin Raymond Hastings shown here in his early thirties operating the Cletrac, the first tractor purchased by Maplewood Farm. This photograph was taken during the excavation for the foundation of
the Boylston Men's Club, which later became the Boylston Town House located at 599 Main Street.
Volunteers constructed the building with funds raised in the local community. The Hastings played a
large role in the project. The club contained two candlepin bowling alleys and a kitchen on the lower
floor. The main floor contained a large hall seating three hundred people and a theatrical stage, complete
with a rear film projection and lighting booth. The building was the sight of the famous 1950s *Reviews*
produced by former vaudevillian and Boylston resident Harry Souci, and Joyce and Russell Fuller. The
annual and special town meetings were also held there.

Will gave his son, Calvin, a REO touring car on his twenty-fifth birthday, but Will remained comfortable with horse and wagon. Calvin's teenage years were filled with hard work, but with that came prosperity as part of a well-to-do family by the standards of the day. The first truck purchased by the farm was also a REO.

(From Worcester County Massachusetts Memoirs, Volume 1–11, *Worcester Telegram, Worcester, Massachusetts, 1908).*

"William Henry Hastings, the principal subject of this sketch, was born in Boylston January 27, 1860, the son of Eli Hastings and the former Adelade Maynard. William acquired his education in the Boylston Public Schools. As a young man he engaged in the live-stock business, which he followed with gratifying success for a number of years, or until unable to compete with the western cattle shippers, and he then engaged in farming exclusively. For two years he served as an assessor, and is at the present time chairman of the Overseers of the Poor. In politics he is a Republican. He is heartily in sympathy with all movements relative to the general improvement of the community, and is an active member of the local Grange, Patrons of Husbandry. In his religious belief he is a Congregationalist. After retiring from the live-stock business Mr. Hastings has engaged extensively in market gardening, the growing of apples and conducts an extensive dairy farm."

The same article noted, "Will's father Eli was a very prosperous farmer in his day. He served in the local militia company. In his earlier years he was a noted cattle dealer in that section, but the active period of his life has, for the most part, been devoted to tilling the soil. He formerly took an interest in civic affairs, serving as road commissioner for a number of terms."

Chapter 11

CALVIN AND ELSA

Anders Brandt was born in 1869 in Bralanda, a small farming community on Sweden's west coast. His parents, Andreas Andresson Brandt and Johanna Anderson, and their forebears before them were tenant farmers. Anders worked on his parents' farm in his youth. In the 1890s a smallpox epidemic in Sweden caused over half a million people to leave the country, many of them immigrating to the United States. Anders Brandt was among them. He entered the United States through the Port of New York on March 8, 1892. Anders was twenty-three years old. He made his way to Worcester where a large population of Swedes had settled and found work at the American Steel and Wire Company, where his trade was listed as that of a wiredrawer.

Maria Nyquist was born in Sweden in 1871 and immigrated to America in 1895 with her parents; her sisters, Louise, Emma, and Anna; and her brother, Pher. The women were employed as domestics in Worcester. Pher worked in a printing office. The Nyquists settled in a three-decker on Belmont Hill, home to a large Swedish population. The Trinity Lutheran Church sponsored them there. Anders Brandt had also located in that neighborhood and had the same church affiliation. Anders met Maria through the church social circle. They were married in Worcester on February 6, 1897.

Elsa Margaret Brandt was born in 1906, the third of Maria and Anders's four children. Elsa had two older brothers Ernest and Ragnar, and a younger brother Robert. She was enrolled in elementary school in Worcester and also attended a Swedish school whose primary aim was to preserve the Swedish language among the children of Swedish immigrants. Following elementary school she graduated from Commerce

High School in Worcester. She then enrolled in and graduated from the Hahnemann Hospital School of Nursing. The Commonwealth of Massachusetts licensed her as a registered nurse.

In the early 1930s, Anders, Maria, and their children moved from Worcester and rented a farmhouse in Boylston, located on School Street next to the Boylston Consolidated School. Maria's sisters and brother remained in the Belmont Hill apartment. Ragner Brandt married immediately after the family moved to Boylston and settled in Winchester, Massachusetts and became a banker. Ernest remained in Boylston and married Agnes Nord. He worked at the Norton Company in Worcester. Robert married Beatrice Wykes and returned to live in Worcester and worked at the American Steel and Wire Company. After nursing school Elsa lived with her parents in the School Street house.

In 1931, the Boylston Girl Scout Troop was planning a two-week camp outing at Laurel Lake in Fitzwilliam, New Hampshire. The scout leader needed an additional chaperone, and the fact that Elsa Brandt was a registered nurse made the choice even easier. The job paid twenty dollars a week, and Elsa was happy to say yes.

Will Hastings volunteered to provide transportation for the Scouts. He asked his son Calvin to take the REO truck and drive the group to Fitzwilliam. The trip took three hours each way.

The REO, usually used for shipping apples to Boston, was refitted with benches on either side of the truck's platform bed, and a canvas was added overhead.

The Maplewood truck with Calvin Hastings at the wheel was parked next to the Common in the center of town. When all the girl scouts were loaded and had bid farewell to their parents, the scout leader climbed in back with the girls and sent Elsa to sit up front with Calvin in the cab.

On that sunny and gentle August morning, as the REO wound its way north on tree-lined country roads, Elsa Brandt had just turned twenty-five. Cal Hastings would turn thirty-one that October.

Elsa Margaret Brandt a year before she married Calvin Hastings at Willard Brook State Park in Ashby, Massachusetts, where the young couple often picnicked on Sunday afternoon outings in the Reo Touring Car.

(Author's note: Marianna Hastings, Elsa's daughter, recalled a conversation with her mother.)

"I fell in love with your father on the day I met him. I talked and your Dad listened. He wanted to know about me. He asked about Commerce High School and why I chose to be a nurse. He laughed when I spoke a few words in Swedish. He had forgotten to bring lunch, but I was happy to share mine."

Rheumatic fever was common in the 1930s. A year after Elsa and Calvin met he contracted the disease for the second time. Will and Melinda needed help in caring for their son. They hired Elsa as a private-duty nurse.

(Author's note: Marianna Hastings remembered her mother's words.)

"Calvin was a very sick young man by the time I arrived at Maplewood Farm. He was running a high fever, had lost weight, and couldn't stand without assistance. I used cold compresses on his body until the fever broke."

Calvin recovered completely, regaining his strength and energy. When Calvin wasn't working at Maplewood, he was with Elsa Brandt, not in the REO truck but driving his REO Touring Car.

Elsa Brandt was a beautiful woman of five feet eight inches. She was outgoing and, like Calvin, had a sense of humor and infectious laugh. Calvin stood six feet two inches with dark hair, was fit from his daily routine on the farm, and was handsome with a quiet personality. Elsa never dated another man or Calvin another woman.

Elsa Margaret Brandt and Calvin Raymond Hastings were married on September 4, 1934, at the First Congregational Church in Fitzwilliam, New Hampshire. Fitzwilliam was the destination that had brought them together two years earlier.

The wedding party standing in front of the Congregational Church at Fitzwilliam, New Hampshire. Rear (left to right): Will Hastings, Calvin Hastings, and Anders Brandt. Front (left to right): Melinda Hastings, Elsa Hastings, and Maria Brandt.

The honeymooners packed the REO and headed to the LaHave Islands in Nova Scotia, Canada, the birthplace of Calvin's mother, Melinda Anastasia Tumblin. Following an arduous journey, mostly on dirt roads in Canada (referenced in family lore as the Rocky Road to Dublin), they stayed on Covey Island with Calvin's third cousin Sadie Wolfe and her husband, Roscoe. Sadie was also from the Tumblin family.

Calvin and Elsa roamed the beautiful island, which except for the gulls they had all to themselves. Their room on the second floor of the Wolfe's clapboard Victorian house looked out to sea past the Mosher's Head lighthouse. They were often awakened by the low moan of a horn signaling that dense fog had crept in, which then would disappear by midmorning. Sadie and Roscoe were also newlyweds and were thrilled to have company at their remote island home. Visiting with friends and relatives was a ritual, as were long walks along the rocky shoreline at dusk.

Ralph Tumblin, Melinda Hastings's older brother, standing before his fish house on Tumblin Island, Nova Scotia. The barrels are for storing herring like those he is holding in his hand.

When the honeymoon was over, Elsa and Calvin returned to Boylston and moved in with Anders and Maria Brandt at their home on School Street. A year later their first child, Calvin Brandt Hastings, was born.

Elsa's knowledge of nursing would play a wider role in Boylston.

(Author's note: My sister, Marianna, shared with me details of Elsa's service to neighbors. Although all of Elsa and Calvin's children were born at Hahnemann Hospital in Worcester, not all families in Boylston were as fortunate. Marianna recalled, "I remember one night the telephone rang very late in the evening. Mom came to me and said, 'Dad and I will be back in a while. You and your brother watch over Gordon while we are gone.' I later learned that Mom and Dad were off to help with the home birth of a neighbor's child. Mom was also often sought out to help people suffering from emotional distress. I believe they turned to Mom because she was a nurse and also a thoughtful listener.")

Chapter 12

THE GREAT DEPRESSION

In the year 1929 the hard times brought on by the Great Depression did not immediately come to Maplewood Farm. Will, an optimist, continued to invest in expansion. He believed in himself and was determined to leave a successful and prosperous Maplewood Farm to his son Calvin just as his father Eli had done for him. He formed a regional dairy cooperative in which he was the major stockholder to try to shore up milk prices. Between 1929 and 1933, milk prices had dropped more than half. Will purchased new equipment, and expanded the milking herd.

With the coming of electricity, Melinda enjoyed the benefits of refrigeration, an early electric mixer, a toaster, and a clothes washing machine. Then came the telephone, the first in their end of town, used as much by neighbors as themselves. A new electrified milk room was added on the front of the barn that included large refrigeration tanks to keep milk cool before being trucked to market. The future still seemed bright for Will, Melinda, and their son Calvin.

The depression worsened, but the plight of the small New England farm was dwarfed compared to those out of work in the cities and in the West who were stricken not only by the depression but also the Dust Bowl. The government instituted programs to help the plains farmers and formed work programs such as the Works Progress Administration to employ out-of-work industrial workers. The government did nothing to recognize the economic hardship being realized at New England family-owned dairy farms such as Maplewood.

By the mid-1930s farm and produce prices had again dropped dramatically. The demand for apples in England vanished, and milk prices were at an all-time low. For the first time in farming history, it cost more to produce the milk than it could be sold for. The milk cooperative that Will organized and helped finance failed, and the banks demanded a return of their investment capital. Unemployment in nearby Worcester and Boston was high, and the prices for all farm goods plummeted. The only good news was that the Hastings were able to produce their own plentiful supply of food, which was shared with family, friends, and neighbors.

Will became more and more realistic as the Great Depression deepened. Despite his and Calvin's enormous efforts, Maplewood Farm, which had reached its zenith under his stewardship, was now in serious jeopardy. As the fifth generation of Hastings to farm land in Boylston and the seventh living in the New World, Will faced personal failure and financial ruin.

William Hastings was a proud individual and examined all options to save Maplewood. There was no market for farmland, so selling off some of the property would not help. The price of milk was so low that the market for a dairy herd was non-existent. Selling the cows for beef was out of the question.

Calvin was not in any position to rescue the farm, as all of his resources were already tied to Maplewood. He also had an infant son and a wife. Will's older sons, Earl and Lee, had gone their own way, and neither possessed the financial resources to help.

In 1933, Will had the foresight to carve out three acres on the western edge of the property at Central and Cross Streets along with the forty-acre south pasture on Cross Street and deeded it to Calvin and Elsa. Because of Will's foresight, at least part of Maplewood Farm would remain in the possession of the Hastings family, and everyone, including him and Melinda, would have a place to live and enough ground from which to harvest a family food supply.

In 1937 Will Hastings's beloved Maplewood Farm was sold to the Aronson brothers of Westborough, Massachusetts. The brothers immediately ceased operating the dairy, apple and the commercial market garden. They closed the main barn, used the fields for summer pasture for dry cattle, and rented the farmhouse to transient families.

They were clearly making an investment in the future value of the land, which less than twenty years later would prove to have been a wise financial decision.

A year later Calvin Raymond Hastings, who had been born and raised in a family of farmers who had worked the land since 1734, became a factory worker employed at the Bay State Abrasives Company in Westborough. The company was hiring more employees as it increased production of grinding wheels in preparation for the military build-up to World War II.

Chapter 13

QUABBIN

By the mid-1930s, the Wachusett Reservoir in Boylston was no longer adequate to fill the demand for water of the growing city of Boston. Boston needed an additional supply of fresh water at the very same time Calvin Hastings needed a house for his family. The confluence of events came at an opportune time for the Hastings.

The Swift River Valley, thirty miles west of Boylston, was to be flooded to make way for the new Quabbin Reservoir. Several towns were to be unincorporated and flooded in exactly the same manner that had spelled the demise of Sawyer's Village in Boylston and appropriated the original Nathaniel Hastings homestead when the Wachusett Reservoir was built in 1895.

One of those communities to be flooded was Enfield, Massachusetts. Rather than demolishing all the homes, the Commonwealth of Massachusetts purchased them and then resold them to anyone who would agree to remove the building.

Homes from Enfield, Massachusetts were moved as far away as Staten Island, New York.

The bill of sale for the Beale home in Enfield, Massachusetts, which was purchased by Calvin Hastings and moved to Central and Cross Streets in Boylston and reconstructed as the new Hastings homestead. Maplewood-Lee.

Calvin's half-brother Eli (Lee) learned about the properties for sale at the future Quabbin reservoir site. Calvin and Lee drove the thirty-five miles to Enfield and found what they saw as the perfect house. It had five bedrooms, two bathrooms, a kitchen, a dining room, a living room, and a center hall with a reversing open interior balcony and staircase connecting the two floors. Each room had colonial wainscoting. There were two fireplaces, one in the dining room, the second in the living room each with a carved soapstone mantelpiece. Calvin purchased the house for $50 upon the condition that it would be removed from the site within ninety days.

The Enfield house was disassembled board by board, and after dozens of trips in the REO stake body truck, the house was ready to be reassembled in Boylston. It was reconstructed on the three acres of Maplewood Farm at the corner of Cross and Central Streets. Lee was an expert carpenter. Calvin Hastings once told his oldest son, "Your Uncle Lee reconstructed the house from memory with no drawings or blueprints." Keeping with the family tradition, a maple tree was planted in the yard in honor of Calvin Brandt Hastings birth. Later, two additional maples were planted, one for Marianna and another for Gordon. The new house was named "Maplewood Lee."

Calvin and Elsa and their newborn son had at last a home of their own but the luxury would not last long. They moved there in 1937. A few months later Maplewood Farm was sold and Will and Melinda, now in their seventies, the patriarch and matriarch of Maplewood Farm, came to live with their son and his wife. A multigenerational cycle dating back to the 1600s was repeated again.

Will Hastings with grandson Calvin Brandt Hastings. The Maplewood farmhouse is in the background. This photo was taken in 1937, a year before Will's death. Calvin had just turned three years old.

William H. Hastings died at Maplewood Lee in 1938 at age seventy-eight. The cause is listed as a hemorrhage after an operation to remove a growth in the bladder. Melinda died at Maplewood Lee less than a year later.

Marianna Hastings was born on October 31, 1937. Gordon Henry Hastings was born on October 17, 1941. Just after Melinda died in 1939, Elsa's mother and father, Anders and Maria Brandt, moved into Maplewood Lee, again continuing the family heritage dating back to the seventeenth century of elderly parents living with their adult children. All of Maplewood Lee's five bedrooms were filled. Maria died in 1942. Anders lived there until his death in 1948.

Anders Brandt in 1945 with his grandson Gordon, age four, shelling peas from the family garden at Maplewood Lee. Note Anders's ever-present pocket watch chain.

In the winter of 1948, the family dog, Pal, was credited with saving a stranger's life during a severe blizzard. Pal's furious barking awakened Calvin in the middle of the night and led him outside to find a woman lying in a deep snow drift making a barely audible call for help. Her name was Beth Cotter. After finishing a late work shift in Worcester, she had set out in the storm to retrieve her eleven-year-old son, Johnnie, who was staying at the nearby Stark Farm on Cross Street. Her old Oldsmobile became stuck. She abandoned the car and attempted to crawl to the house, nearly succumbing to exhaustion. Following Pal's furious barking through the wind blown snow, Calvin found her half buried in a deep drift. He carried her inside and after several days of Elsa's expert nursing care her strength was restored. She had nearly died of hypothermia.

Neither Calvin nor Elsa had met Beth Cotter before that fateful night. Later that same winter the neighboring Stark Farm barn and fifty head of cattle were destroyed in a pre-dawn fire. Beth Cotter came to the Hastings and asked Calvin and Elsa if Johnnie could stay with them until she resettled. They agreed to help, and Johnnie became a member of the Hastings family for two and a half years.

Life in Boylston in the 1940s and early 1950s was mostly bucolic. Neighbors made up the social life for the adults and playmates for the children. Adult activities, including backyard picnics, were organized to involve the neighborhood children. The Garfield's, who lived across Central Street in a centuries-old farmhouse, owned the only cow and horse in the neighborhood since Maplewood Farm was sold. They kept a cow for their family milk supply and a horse named Molly to cultivate their vegetable garden and bring in the annual harvest of hay for winter fodder. Filled with anticipation and excitement, each year all the neighborhood children would join Grandpa (Joseph) Garfield aboard an old hay wagon pulled by Molly for the trip to the hayfield on Cross Street. Calvin borrowed Molly to cultivate the Hastings large garden.

Heavy winter snowstorms were common in Boylston in the 1940s. From left to right: Johnnie Cotter, Cal, Gordon, and Marianna standing in front of Maplewood Lee. This was the first winter that Johnnie came to live with the Hastings family.

Cal, Gordon, and the family dog, Pal, aboard the wagon used to haul wood from the south pasture family woodlot. Pal is credited with saving Beth Cotter's life during a blizzard in 1948.

The Hastings at Maplewood Lee did not own a manufactured tractor, but rather Calvin with the help of his son built one from an old Model A Ford truck by cutting off the cab, shortening the frame, and arranging a hitch on the rear to pull a wagon, single-blade plow, and field harrow. These homemade tractors were often called Doodlebugs. This 1944 photograph shows Marianna at the wheel of the Doodlebug with Gordon. The farmhouse and barn occupied by Earl and Edna Hastings can be seen through the corn in the background. The second Nathaniel and his wife, Betsy, first occupied this house in the early 1800s when he bought the original property constituting the beginning of Maplewood Farm.

Grandpa Garfield's horse, Molly, with all the neighborhood children in 1945 in the driveway of Maplewood Lee. Seated on Molly (left to right): Paul Pratt, Cal, and Gordon. Standing (left to right): Marianna and Carol Garfield.

The family double-runner bobsled built by Eli Hastings in the 1880s. The giant sled, which could carry up to twelve children, was as thrilling to them as a modern roller coaster is to children today.

The Hastings family in 1953 ready to depart on the long sought after family trip to Nova Scotia, Canada. The 1949 Pontiac Silver Streak was acquired after years of saving to make the three-day journey. Left to right: Calvin, Elsa, Marianna, and Gordon. Cal, not shown, took the photograph.

Calvin and Elsa in 1953 at Covey Island, Nova Scotia, Canada. This was their first and last trip to Nova Scotia since going there on their honeymoon in 1934. Elsa died a year later.

In an ironic twist, just as had happened to his grandfather, Eli, Calvin's wife, Elsa, tragically died of a cerebral hemorrhage in 1954, leaving him to raise their three children. Also like his grandfather, he never remarried and assumed the full responsibility of raising the children alone. Calvin R. Hastings died of lung cancer in 1963 at age sixty-three. He had worked at Bay State Abrasives for twenty-five years. Calvin served for many years as a deacon and trustee of the First Congregational Church. He also served several terms as a town of Boylston assessor.

BAY STATE ABRASIVE PRODUCTS CO.
WESTBORO, MASSACHUSETTS

ARTHUR E. GILMAN
PRESIDENT

January 2, 1963

Mr. Gordon Hastings
Main Street
Boylston, Mass.

Dear Gordon:

We are shocked and saddened at the sudden death of your father on New Year's Day. Cal Hastings and I started at Bay State within a couple years of each other. Over the years I've come to know, like and respect him both as a man and as an employee.

He was a man of conscience and deep conviction, and his contribution to this company in his very specialized work has been substantial. His interest and work in his church is known to us all.

His passing is a personal loss to those who knew him as well as a loss to his community and this company. My deepest sympathy to you and to the other members of your family.

Sincerely,

Arthur Gilman

President

AEGilman/S

A tribute to Calvin Hastings from Arthur Gillman, President of Bay State Abrasives.

Chapter 14

CONCLUSION

Maplewood Lee, the home built by Calvin and Elsa Hastings at the intersection of Cross and Central Streets, remains as of this writing. Gordon H. Hastings was the last Hastings to live there. All the other original buildings of Maplewood Farm, including the Silas Hastings house on Green Street, have been removed. The Daniel Hastings house on Central Street remains. The remainder of the Maplewood Farm property with the exception of the thirty-eight-acre south pasture was sold to the Aronson Brothers of Westborough in 1937. The hurricane of 1938 destroyed a majority of the Maplewood Farm apple orchards, some of which were originally planted by Nathaniel Hastings in the 1800s. The beautiful maple trees along Central Street survived the hurricane.

Following the 1953 Worcester, Massachusetts, tornado in which one of the Aronson brothers was killed at his farm in Westborough, the Aronsons sold the Maplewood Farm property to a group of private individuals from Worcester who formed a corporation and built the original Mt. Pleasant Golf and Country Club. The country club incorporated all the Maplewood Farm land and buildings on Central Street and Stiles Road and the land belonging to the former Stark Farm on Cross Street. For many years the old Central Street farmhouse built by Eli was the home of the country club greens keeper. The main Maplewood Farm barn across the street was used for equipment storage. Later, both of the structures were torn down.

Upon his death, the estate of Calvin R. Hastings was divided equally among his children, Calvin B. Hastings, Marianna Hastings Canovitch, and Gordon H. Hastings.

Calvin and Gordon through an arrangement with Marianna purchased her share of the Boylston real estate.

Gordon H. Hastings took title to the house and land at Cross-and Central Streets called Maplewood Lee. He served two terms in the 1960s as Town of Boylston Treasurer, as had his great-great-great-great-great-grandfather, Silas, from 1823 to 1832. He was also a well-known radio news announcer at station WAAB in Worcester and rose to the position of general manager of the radio station. He lived in Boylston until 1972, when he sold the property and moved to New York City, where he became president and director of Katz Media Corporation and later formed Hastings Broadcasting Corporation. He also founded the Broadcasters Foundation of America, a nonprofit organization serving broadcasters in need.

Marianna Hastings married Lowell Canovitch of Haverhill, Massachusetts, shortly before her father died and became a resident of Haverhill. Following her mother's passion for helping others, she established herself in a career spanning five decades in nursing and public health. The state of Massachusetts Department of Health presented her with the Outstanding Outreach Educator Award. She was cited for special recognition by the city of Lawrence, Massachusetts: "Marianna Hastings for the loving care provided for the Senior Citizens of Lawrence." She coauthored a program funded by the National Institutes of Health for Spanish-speaking people suffering from diabetes. The program received national recognition and remains in use at this writing.

Calvin B. Hastings purchased from his father's estate the thirty-eight acres on Cross Street, which was the south pasture of the early Maplewood Farm and later became the family woodlot. In the 1970s he constructed a home there where he lived until 2002, when he sold the property and moved to Nahant, Massachusetts. For many years he operated Horne and Hastings Real Estate from offices located at Main Street and French Drive in Boylston. He also established Bay Path, a development of commodious family homes on property off Central Street and adjacent to the former Maplewood Farm south pasture. Calvin served as a trustee of the Boylston Congregational Church in the 1980s and 90s. He was also among the stalwarts of the acclaimed Boylston Congregational Church Choir, performances of which were noted with great praise throughout the area in the 1960s to 1980s. He was a professional tenor soloist singing with church choirs throughout Worcester County and a soloist with the Worcester Chorus and the Worcester Oratorical Society.

Calvin was the last of the direct descendants of Nathanial and Esther Hastings to reside in Boylston. He left there in 2002. It had been 268 years since Nathaniel and his wife arrived in Boylston in 1734.

At this writing, the family is dispersed but remains largely in New England. Calvin B. Hastings and his wife, Marrit Nauta Hastings, live in Massachusetts, as do Marianna Hastings Canovitch and her husband, Lowell. Gordon H. Hastings and his wife, Lynn Daly Hastings, reside in Connecticut. The grandchildren and great-grandchildren of Calvin and Elsa Brandt Hastings reside in Massachusetts, Connecticut, Maine, and New York. Descendents of Thomas Hastings have resided in Massachusetts for 382 consecutive years.

(Author's note: Gordon H. Hastings's memoir, Rocky Road to Dublin, *set to be published in 2017, details his life in Boylston from childhood in the 1940s through his young adulthood in the 1960s. It will be available in both print and digitally at Amazon.com.)*

HASTINGS GENEALOGY

Thomas Hastings
B. East Anglia, England, 1605, D. Watertown, Massachusetts, 1685
M. Susannah Woodward B. 1600, D. 1650
M. Margaret Cheney (1651). B. 1628, D. 1678

Samuel Hastings
B. 1665, D. Watertown, Massachusetts, 1723
M. Sara Coolidge (1701). B. 1678, D. 1724

Nathaniel Hastings
B. Watertown, Massachusetts, 1710, D. Boylston, Massachusetts, 1789
M. Esther Perry (1734). B. 1713, D. Unknown

Silas Hastings
B. 1746, D. 1833
M. Hannah Reed (est. 1776). B. 1756, D. 1843

Nathaniel Hastings
B. 1797, D. 1854
M. Betsy Eager Hastings (1821) B. 1801, D. 1874

Eli Hastings
B. 1830, D. 1906
M. Adelade Maynard (1856). B. 1836, D. 1887

William Henry Hastings
B. 1860, D. 1938
M. Arvilla Snow (1885). B. 1866, D. 1894
M. Melinda Tumblin (1895). B. 1869, D. 1939

Calvin Raymond Hastings
B. 1900, D. 1963
M. Elsa Margaret Brandt (1934). B. 1906, D. 1954

Calvin Brandt Hastings
B. July 1934
M. Marjorie Horne (1959)
M. Marrit Nauta (June 1992)

Erik Hastings (B. April 1975)
M. Megan Higgins (May, 2004)

Parker Alexander Hastings
B. June 2006

Griffin Taylor Hastings
B. April 2009

-0-
Marianna Hastings
B. October 1937
M. Lowell Anthony Canovitch (1961)

Cynthia Dawn Canovitch
B. March 1963

Jeffrey Hastings Canovitch
B. August 1965, D. October 1995

Cynthia Dawn Canovitch
M. Paul Findeis (October 1990)

Benjamin Lowell Findeis
B. December 1993

Alexander Jeffrey Findeis
B. August 1997

-0-

Gordon Henry Hastings
B. October 1941
M. Penelope Brown (1961)

Dwight Sanford Hastings
B. June 1963

M. Christine Marie Moody (October 2000)

Meghan Christine Hastings
B. August 2002

Jonathan Dwight Hastings
B. October 2005

Gordon Calvin Hastings (B. May, 1966)
M. Catherine Ragan O'Malley (November 1991)

Calla Margrete Hastings
B. August 1992

Aedan Grace Hastings
B. June 1996
Liam Henry Hastings
B. April 2001

-0-

Gordon Henry Hastings
M. Lynn Ann Daly (April 1978)

Brandt Daly Hastings
B. January 1980
Alexandra Catherine Hastings
B. September 1985

Brandt Daly Hastings
M. Brooke Wigton (October 2009)

Charlotte Trewin Hastings
B. December 2012

Margaret Whitney Hastings
B. April 2014

Appendix

BURIAL GROUNDS

The Boylston Historical Society has catalogued all the graves in the Old Boylston Cemetery and the Pine Grove Cemetery. By visiting their website, the user can view photos of most of the gravestones and their inscriptions.

There is no grave for Daniel Hastings or his wife, Sarah, who came to Boylston in 1724. There is no gravesite identified for either Nathaniel or his wife, Esther, who came to Boylston in 1734.

Nathaniel and Esther may have been buried in a family plot on their original property located on an old pathway moving east from Hastings Cove on the Wachusett Reservoir across Route 70. The unmarked graves may still be there but were not reported upon inspection of the old foundations by Calvin B. Hastings, Dwight S. Hastings, and Lowell Canovitch in the 1990s. It would be unusual for a large family burial ground not to be found. The graves could possibly be under water because much of the original Nathanial Hastings property was flooded in 1906 when the Nashua River was dammed, creating the Wachusett Reservoir. There is no record of those graves being identified and moved when the Wachusett Reservoir was constructed.

Nathaniel and Esther had six children including Silas Hastings, the father of the second Nathaniel. There is no recorded grave in Boylston for Silas or his wife, Hannah.

Several different reasons for the missing graves are possible.

Between the two original Hastings couples to settle in Boylston, Nathaniel and Esther and Daniel and Sarah, there were a total of sixteen children, and of these progeny, only one grave has been identified in the Old Boylston Cemetery. Daniel and Sarah Ball's child Stephen, born in August 1727, is buried there. A generation later Silas and Hannah's youngest child, Silas Hastings Jr., born in 1780 and died in 1833, is buried there beneath a marker. This is the Silas who owned and operated the Hastings Tavern in Boylston Center.

(Author's note: Boylston was located in the North Precinct of Shrewsbury until it was incorporated as a town in 1786. It is possible that some of the children are buried in graveyards in Shrewsbury; a search of Worcester County cemeteries found over five hundred Hastings burials, but none of them was the direct ancestors of Nathaniel Hastings. When the Wachusett Reservoir was constructed, all the graves in the flooded valley and surrounding watershed taken for the project were relocated by the MDC. It would seem that if any Hastings graves were relocated, the MDC authorities would have contacted William H. Hastings at Maplewood Farm. There is no record of that occurring, either in writing or anecdotally.)

The Boylston Historical Society offers some additional insight on its website as to the status of burials in the Old Boylston Cemetery.

(Author's note: Due to the loss of earlier burial records prior to 1747, it is impossible to know for certain the burials here, except those where gravestones were placed. This is in reference to the Old Cemetery on School Street. It could very well be that Daniel and Betsy and Nathaniel and Esther and some of their children are interred there.)

In summary the missing graves are as follows: Daniel and Sarah Hastings and Nathaniel and Esther Hastings. Only one of Daniel and Sarah's children, Stephen, is buried in the Old Boylston Cemetery. The burial places of the remaining fifteen children are unknown. Skipping a generation, Silas Jr., son of Silas and Hannah Reed Hastings, is the only other direct family member buried with a marker in the Old Boylston Cemetery.

The Pine Grove Cemetery on Scar Hill Road was opened in 1837. Hastings family burials there are well recorded and marked, beginning with the gravestones of Nathaniel

and Betsy Hastings. A headstone inscription on this plot may confuse future generations. The name "Horne" that appears on the stone is the maiden name of Calvin B.
Hastings's first wife, Marjorie Horne. As an act of kindness, Calvin B. Hastings autho-
rized his father-in-law, Archie J. Horne, to be buried there. Later, the same authoriza-
tion was made for the burial of Archie Horne's wife, Marion.

The original Hastings lot at the Pine Grove Cemetery is in the northernmost section of the cemetery, Section 1, Lot 51. The following graves are located there unless
otherwise noted.

Nathaniel Hastings, 1797–1854
Betsy Eager Hastings, 1801–1874

Nathaniel and Betsy's children:
Lucy, 1822–1885 (buried under a marker of her husband, Henry Calvin Hastings)
Martha Ann, 1827–1828
Dolly Hastings Sanderson (Eli's sister)
Sophia Hastings Fales
Dolly Louise Hastings

Eli Hastings, 1830–1906
Adelade Hastings, 1836–1887

Eli and Adelade's children:
Nathaniel Waldo, 1859–1869
Samuel 1871–1872
Infant, 1873
Charles, 1874–1875
Lottie Hastings Burpee, 1878–1964
Emma Roxanna Hastings Winchester, 1864–1938

Buried in the original plot, Section 1, Lot 73 at Pine Grove Cemetery:
William Henry Hastings, 1860–1938
Arvilla Snow Hastings, 1866–1894
Melinda Tumblin Hastings, 1869–1939

William H. and Arvilla's children:

Eli (Lee) Hastings, 1887–1960

William Earl Hastings 1890–1965 (Buried in a separate plot, Section 1, Lot 50, un-marked grave. Also buried there are his wife, Edna Hastings, and daughter, Eleanor Arvilla Hastings Pratt, 1917–1943. All the aforementioned graves are unmarked. Earl and Edna's son, William S. Hastings, 1915–1975, is also buried in Section 1, Lot 50. There is a marker for his grave along with that of his wife, Clara Whitcomb Hastings, 1910–1996.

William H. and Melinda's children:

William Albert Hastings, 1896 Infant

Also buried here at the request of William Hastings is Arvilla's younger brother, Lehman Snow, who died at age twenty-eight in 1899.

Buried in second Hastings plot, Section 2, Lot 261 midsection, Pine Grove Cemetery:

Elsa Brandt Hastings, 1906–1954

Calvin Raymond Hastings, 1900–1963

An infant child buried there with a grave marker is that of Calvin B. and Marjorie Hastings.

Headstone Brandt/Nyquist plot, Section 2, Lot 262, Pine Grove Cemetery:

Anders Brandt, 1869–1948

Maria Brandt, 1870–1942

Also buried in this plot:

Louise Nyquist (Maria's sister), 1874–1952

Pher G. Nyquist (Maria's brother), 1878–1962

Made in the USA
Middletown, DE
01 September 2018